Inhaltsverzeichni

Inhaltsangabe

Die Journalistin Carol Ford will eine längere Film-Reportage über das Schlittenhundrennen „Nordic Wilderness Race“ drehen. Da sie vermutet, dass es bei dem Rennen nicht mit rechten Dingen zugeht, bittet sie die drei ???, ihr bei dem Dreh zu helfen und sich gleichzeitig vor Ort als Detektive umzuschauen.
Justus, Peter und Bob vermuten, dass einer der Teilnehmer des Rennens seine Konkurrenten sabotiert, um das Preisgeld zu gewinnen. Zudem kommt es in der alten Goldgräberstadt Dawson auch noch zu einem Einbruch in das Museum. Ein Goldschatz von großem Wert wird gestohlen.
Gemeinsam mit der Journalistin Carol fahren die Jungen auf Schneemobilen in die verschneite Wildnis von Alaska. Schon bald kommt es zu Unfällen unter den Rennteilnehmern.
Als Carol und Peter den Schlittenhunden eines Nachts auf einem Motorschlitten folgen, kommt es zu einem lebensgefährlichen Zwischenfall auf einem zugefrorenen Fluss.
Können die drei ??? rechtzeitig rausfinden, wer hinter der Sabotage steckt? Und können sie den Dieb des Goldes überführen?
Die drei ??? haben alle Hände voll zu tun, um diesen eiskalten Fall zu lösen!

Auftretende Personen

Justus Jonas:
Justus ist der Anführer der drei ???. Seit dem frühen Tod seiner Eltern lebt er bei seiner Tante und seinem Onkel in der kalifornischen Küstenstadt Rocky Beach. Justus ist überdurchschnittlich intelligent und betreibt gerne Denksport. Mit anderen Sportarten kann er weniger anfangen. Er ist leicht übergewichtig.

Peter Shaw:
Peter ist der zweite Detektiv. Er ist sehr sportlich, hochgewachsen und fast immer gut gelaunt. Im Gegensatz zu Justus ist Peter nicht ganz überzeugt, dass es für alle Phänomene eine logische Erklärung gibt. Daher ist er lieber etwas vorsichtig, wenn es um unheimliche Ereignisse geht.

Bob Andrews:
Bob ist bei den drei ??? für Recherchen und Archiv zuständig. Das bedeutet, dass er in der Bibliothek und im Internet Informationen sammelt und die Fälle der drei ??? dokumentiert. Bob ist sehr gewissenhaft. Er interessiert sich für Rockmusik und liest gerne.

Carol Ford:
Carol ist eine junge Journalistin und arbeitet für einen Fernsehsender. Sie kennt die drei ??? durch Bobs Vater, der ebenfalls Journalist ist.

Francis Studstill:
Francis ist eine Hundeschlittenführerin aus Alaska. Sie ist klein und drahtig und hat viele Sommersprossen. Sie steht im Mittelpunkt von Carols Reportage.

Jared Fox:
Mr Fox ist auch ein Hundeschlittenführer. Er ist abergläubisch und hat in der Wildnis angeblich schon Gnome und Hexen gesehen.

Candace Jane Duskin:
Die hübsche junge Hundeschlittenführerin nimmt ebenfalls am Rennen teil.

Baxter Norsworthy:
Der Hundeschlittenführer liebt es im Mittelpunkt zu stehen und nimmt wenig Rücksicht auf andere. Er will das Rennen unbedingt gewinnen.

Mr Woodland:
Der ältere Mann ist ein reicher Fabrikant und hat dem Museum von Dawson einen Goldschatz für die Ausstellung ausgeliehen. Er ist außerdem einer der Sponsoren des Rennens.

Duane Carpenter:
Der Fotograf aus Anchorage begleitet Carol und die drei ??? bei ihrer Reportage. Doch es scheint so, als habe er ein Geheimnis.

Jelena Charcova:
Jelena ist eine gute Freundin von Bob. Sie ist sehr schlau und hat den drei ??? in der Vergangenheit schon bei mehreren Fällen geholfen, obwohl sie ständig Streit mit Justus hat. Jelena fährt nicht mit nach Alaska, aber die drei ??? rufen sie an, um Informationen über die Rennteilnehmer zu bekommen.

1. Nice Dogs and bad Cookies

TR. 01

"I'm cold!" says Peter Shaw.
"Me too!" agrees Bob Andrews.
"But here in Dawson it's only ten degrees[1] below zero!" says Justus Jonas. "When we go to Alaska, it will be much colder! In the wilderness you get temperatures up to thirty degrees below zero!"
The Three Investigators[2] from California have just arrived in Canada. Now they are on their way to a meeting with Carol Ford. The reporter is a friend of Bob's father. The Three Investigators already worked for her some months ago. Now Carol Ford has a new job for the boys: She is writing a report on the sled-dog race[3] "Nordic Wilderness Race" and needs a camera team.
"Great you came!" Carol Ford greets the boys. "It's so cold, I feel like a snowman. Or better: a snowwoman! "
"We're glad that we can help you, Carol!" says Justus. He looks around. They are standing by a huge[4] parking area. All the people who take part in the sled-dog race camp here. There is a cabin[5] where you can buy food and a cabin with restrooms[6]. Justus sees a lot of ski-doos[7] and a couple of trucks that have holes in the sides. Dogs are looking out of the holes. People in warm coats are walking across the snowy area. Some are carrying buckets[8] of water, others are loading sleeping bags, lamps and cans onto their sleds. Everyone is busy.
"I really need your help here!" Carol says while they walk towards the trucks.

1 degree: Grad
2 investigator: Ermittler
3 sled-dog race: Schlittenhundrennen
4 huge: riesig
5 cabin: Hütte
6 restroom: Toilette
7 ski-doo: Schneemobil
8 bucket: Eimer

"Well," says Peter, "it's good you need us now! We don't have to go to school this week. You're lucky it's a school-holiday week in California. Besides[1], at the moment we have a lot of time, because we don't have a criminal case[2]."

"I actually[3] have a case for you!" Carol Ford says in a low voice.

"Really? A criminal case?" Suddenly, Justus sounds very happy. The word "case" always has a magical impact[4] on the First Investigator.

"Yes! I think it's sabotage!" says Carol. "Somebody is trying to harm[5] the other mushers!"

"What are mushers?" asks Peter.

"I'm sorry, Carol," says Justus. "Your Second Investigator was sleeping when Bob and I talked about the race on the plane."

"When you talked about the race?" Peter says amused, "You held an endless lecture[6] about sled-dogs and racing rules and the weather in Alaska! After half an hour I really needed a break!"

"Please, don't argue[7] about this now! We do not have much time. The race starts tomorrow. And you need to be prepared[8]!" says Carol. "To make it short: A musher is the person who stands on the sled and controls the dogs."

"There are about twelve to sixteen dogs in front of each sled," Justus Jonas explains.

"I know that!" says Peter. He throws his scarf[9] over his shoulder. "They drive across the marked trail[10] from the Canadian town Dawson

1 besides: außerdem
2 case: Fall
3 actually – *hier*: tatsächlich
4 a magical impact: eine magische Wirkung
5 to harm someone: jemandem schaden
6 lecture – *hier*: Vortrag
7 to argue: streiten, argumentieren
8 prepared: vorbereitet
9 scarf: Schal
10 marked trail: markierter Pfad, markierte Strecke

to Fairbanks in Alaska. I also know that they will start tomorrow at nine o'clock. See! I wasn't asleep the whole time!"
Justus ignores Peter, "Carol, why do you think that there is a saboteur[1]? Can you tell us more?"
"Strange things have happened here. Someone destroyed[2] a sled. Dogs got sick. And then something happened to Francis Studstill and my camera-team!" Carol tells him. She has just finished her sentence, when a young woman steps out of a yellow truck. She is small and has red hair and freckles[3].
"Hello Francis!" says Carol.
"Hi!" The young woman smiles and shakes their hands. Even though Francis is so small and thin, she is very strong! Bob looks at his hand. It aches[4] a little. Peter and Justus also look surprised.
"I'm so happy you found a new team!" Francis says to Carol. "This time I will not offer them any cookies! No way!"
"No cookies?" Peter says with a glance at the First Investigator. "Too bad! Justus Jonas here loves cookies! He cannot get enough of them," Peter laughs.
But Justus Jonas growls[5] and throws an angry glance[6] at his friend. Sure, he does like cookies, but he hates it when other people make fun of him. Actually the First Investigator is a little bit stocky[7].
"Carol's last team became sick when they ate my cookies," Francis tells them. "The doctor says it was food poisoning[8]!"
Justus looks surprised again. "But food poisoning normally happens with meat and raw[9] eggs and not with cookies!"

1 saboteur: Saboteur
2 to destroy: zerstören
3 freckles: Sommersprossen
4 to ache – a different word for *to hurt*
5 to growl: knurren
6 glance: Blick
7 stocky: not thin (stämmig)
8 food poisoning: Lebensmittelvergiftung
9 raw: not cooked (roh)

"It must have been the cookies. It was the only thing Carol and I did not eat that day."
"I'm sure it was an act of sabotage!" Carol Ford says. "Somebody poisoned your cookies, Francis! And then my crew ate them and got sick. They are better now but one of them is still in hospital."
"Well, it really sounds like sabotage!" Bob says.
The musher Francis shakes her head. "I don't believe it! I take part in so many races and nothing like this has ever happened! Sled-dog races are hard but fair! Believe me!"
"Well, there are rumours[1] that somebody is using unfair methods!" Carol tells Francis. She bends over[2] to the musher and says in a low voice: "Your opponent[3] Jared Fox says that somebody tried to break a sled!"
"Jared Fox!" Francis laughs. "He is a strange man! At the "Cross-Alaska Race" he told the reporters: "I've seen monsters! There are monsters and goblins[4] in the forest! With red eyes!" Francis looks amused. "It's funny."
"Does he really believe in monsters?" Peter asks.
"Yes, he does. But it's normal to see strange things in the wilderness. Especially when you don't eat, drink or sleep enough. I bet[5] Jared Fox was just dehydrated when he saw the monsters."
"What does "dehydrated" mean?" Peter asks.
"It means that your body needs water. It happens when you don't drink enough water. That is a real problem for the mushers! On the trail we are often very thirsty and very tired."
"It seems to be a hard journey!" Bob Andrews says. The small Third Investigator rubs[6] snowflakes from his glasses.

1 rumour: Gerücht
2 bend over to someone – *hier:* sich zu jemandem beugen
3 opponent: Gegner
4 goblin – a kind of small monster
5 to bet: wetten
6 to rub: reiben

"It is!" Francis answers. "Who knows what will happen this time. Maybe Jared Fox will get dehydrated again. Maybe he will see yetis[1] or radioactive witches[2]."

"But, – " Justus tries to say something.

"Stop!" Francis says. She holds up both hands. "Don't make me nervous. Not now! I don't want to believe that there is a saboteur! Please boys, let's change the topic. There are nicer things to talk about." She turns to her truck. "Would you like to take a look at my dogs?"

"Yes, please!" Bob Andrews answers.

"These dogs are the best sled-dogs in all of South Alaska!" Francis pats[3] a big grey dog. He barks[4].

Justus takes a step back. "Do they bite?"

Francis laughs and pats another dog. "No. They behave[5] like wolves when I feed them but otherwise[6] they are really tame[7]!"

"May I touch one?" Peter asks. The Second Investigator really likes animals.

"Yes!" Francis points at a black dog with blue eyes. "This is Spooky. He is my youngest dog. He loves to be patted. He won't bite!"

Carefully, Pete pats Spooky. "He is really nice!"

Now, Bob also pats Spooky.

"I can rely on[8] Spooky and the other dogs," Francis says. "And that is really important because we are going to drive more than one hundred miles through the wilderness! That is a long way. We have to cope with[9] the extreme cold, with storms and dangerous situations!"

1 yeti: a white, furry monster that lives in the mountains (Yeti)
2 witch: Hexe
3 to pat – *hier*: tätscheln
4 to bark: bellen
5 to behave like: sich verhalten wie
6 otherwise: ansonsten
7 tame: zahm
8 to rely on: sich verlassen auf
9 to cope with: zurechtkommen mit

Justus still doesn't go near the dogs. Instead he turns to Francis. "Can you tell us something about the other mushers?"
"Why?" she asks.
"We're just curious[1]," Peter says. "As reporters we have to know all about the race! For example the names of the mushers."
"Well, there are five other mushers who qualified[2] for the race: Jared Fox, Curtis Moylan, Candace Jane Duskin, Baxter Norsworthy and Gordon Hoke. Four other mushers cannot take part. Two of them are ill, like Carol's assistants. The others can't take part because their dogs are sick."
"So there are six people now. Who do you think is the best musher?" Justus asks. "Is there a musher who always wins?"
"They are all very good. But I think Baxter Norsworthy has the best dogs. These dogs are quite famous in Alaska and Baxter is famous too. But I don't like him. He is rude and he shows off[3]. Baxter behaves like he is the greatest musher of all time."
"How about the other woman?" Bob asks. "This Candace ... I can't remember her full name."
"Candace Duskin? Well, she works hard to win! She wants to get a contract with one of the sponsors "Kodiak Sports" or "Apollo Dogfood". As you might know, the winner of the race is hired to do advertising[4] for those companies. Of course the companies pay a lot of money for advertising."
"So there's a reason why somebody would sabotage the others!" says Carol. "The winner gets all the money! And you know how some people will do anything[5] for money!"

1 curious: neugierig
2 to qualify: sich qualifizieren (für einen Wettkampf oder einen Job)
3 to show off: angeben
4 is hired to do advertising: wird eingestellt, um Werbung zu machen
5 to do anything for money: alles für Geld tun

"No Carol! That can't be true!" Francis turns to the reporter. "Our real enemies[1] are the snow, the ice and the dangerous animals in the forest. I don't want to believe that I also have to be afraid of the other mushers!"
"You may not think so[2], but please be careful!" Carol says to the musher. "Something is going on here!"

Detective Question 1

What motive *(Beweggrund)* does Carol think the saboteur has?

1 enemy: Feind, Gegner
2 you may not think so: du denkst das vielleicht nicht

2. The Thief

TR. 02

"Why didn't you tell her that you are investigators?" Carol asks when they walk across the parking area. They head towards[1] a group of small cabins.
"I prefer not to tell everybody," Justus explains. "It's much easier for us to investigate[2] when people underestimate[3] us and think that we are just three schoolboys."
"Yes," Bob adds[4], "people mustn't know[5] that we are investigators."
Carol opens the door. The boys read a sign that says: "Press Office[6]". They enter a small room with a table, a small kitchen and a couple of chairs.
"Would you like hot coffee?" Carol asks.
The boys nod[7]. Carol looks for four clean mugs[8]. "I really hate it that nobody believes my sabotage theory!"
"Have you talked to the police, Carol?" Justus asks. He takes off his scarf and his coat.
"Yes, of course," Carol puts some sugar in the mugs. "They launched[9] a short investigation. But they found nothing. The sheriff says that he has more important things to do!" She looks angry. "I know why!

1 to head towards: sich auf etwas zubewegen
2 to investigate: ermitteln
3 to underestimate: unterschätzen
4 to add: hinzufügen
5 mustn't know: dürfen nicht erfahren
6 press office: Pressestelle
7 to nod: nicken
8 mug: Tasse
9 to launch: starten

The police don't want to investigate this case because there is a much bigger case for them."
"Something even bigger than sabotage?" Justus says with an interested voice.
"Somebody broke into the local[1] museum!" Carol tells him.
"Did he steal something?" Peter asks. He takes a sip[2] of coffee. It tastes terrible! Peter nearly spits it back into the mug.
"Yes!" Carol answers. She pauses and looks at the boys. "The thief stole a real treasure[3]: a whole bucket full of gold!"
"What?" The boys are surprised. "A bucket full of gold? Real gold?"
"Yes, real gold and other valuable[4] things!" Carol says. "There is an exhibition[5] on the "Gold Rush" at the museum. They show old pictures of gold-mines, the equipment[6] of gold diggers[7] and also some real nuggets[8]!"
"I read about that in the local paper!" Bob Andrews tells his friends. "The article says that the museum is very proud to show a bag that belonged to Jack London."
"Jack London, the famous writer?" Justus asks. He runs his fingers through his black hair.
"Yes! A rich collector from New York lent it to the museum."
"That stupid robbery!" Carol says. She slams[9] her mug on the table.

1 local: örtlich
2 sip: Schluck
3 treasure: Schatz
4 valuable: wertvoll
5 exhibition: Ausstellung
6 equipment: Ausstattung, Werkzeug
7 gold digger: Goldgräber
8 nugget: Goldklumpen
9 to slam: knallen

"Everybody is talking about the stolen gold and the stolen bag! Hardly anybody[1] cares about the race anymore!"
"Well, this definitely is a very interesting case!" Justus says. "I would like to investigate the robbery! It's interesting that the thief took the gold and the bag. Who wants a simple bag that is more than one hundred years old?"
"There is nothing to investigate!" Carol tells the boys. "The sheriff has a good theory: The thief can't leave Dawson with the gold and this stupid bag."
"Why not?" Bob asks. He takes down notes[2] on a piece of paper.
"The night the robbery took place there was a blizzard," Carol explains.
"You mean a severe[3] storm with a lot of snow?"
"Yes. Nobody was able to drive out of the town. And now the police screens[4] every car that leaves Dawson. It is easy because there are just a few streets that leave town."
"But the thief could leave through the forest!" Justus suggests[5].
"How? I don't think that's possible. There is nothing but snow out there. The next town is far away and it's dangerous to go out there alone. I think the thief has to wait until spring to get away."
"Still, I think it's an interesting case!" Justus mumbles[6].
"Please, remember that you are here to help me!", Carol says. "I need you as assistants and I need you as investigators. That is more than enough. Don't you think so?"

1 hardly anybody: kaum einer
2 to take down notes: Notizen machen
3 severe – *hier*: stark, heftig
4 to screen – *hier*: überprüfen
5 to suggest: vorschlagen
6 to mumble: nuscheln, murmeln

"We won't forget that!" Justus promises[1] and takes a sip of his coffee. He coughs[2]. "Well, that is ..." He looks into his cup, then he looks at Carol. "... nice coffee."
"Liar!" Peter whispers[3].

Detective Question 2

What do you think was the thief's reason to steal an old bag?

1 to promise: versprechen
2 to cough: husten
3 to whisper: flüstern

3. Peter the Psychic[1]

TR. 03

One hour later Bob carries a microphone past a group of journalists.

"Place it right in front of Mr Woodland's face!" Carol shouts. "And hurry up, Bob!"

Carol wants to interview Charles Woodland, one of the sponsors of the race. Mr Woodland is a man in his late fifties[2] and he has a big mustache.

"Mr Woodland," a small reporter shouts, "is it true that you owned[3] one of the gold nuggets that have been stolen?"

The big man sighs[4]. "Yes, it's true. I'm a collector of gold rush artifacts[5]. I lent some valuable items[6] from my collection to the Dawson Museum." He looks very sad. "The thief took my favourite gold nugget. It was a real treasure! A prospector[7] found it in Klondike in 1898."

"Now that you have to cope with your loss[8], will you still let the race go on?" a reporter asks.

"Of course! Actually, when I was younger, I used to be an adventurer[9]. That is why I really like sled-dog races and why my company "Kodiac Sports" supports the "Nordic Wilderness Race". As you all know, "Kodiac Sports" offers warm coats and ..."

1 the psychic: das Medium
2 in his late fifties: Ende fünfzig
3 to own: besitzen
4 to sigh: seufzen
5 artifact: Artefakt, Gegenstand
6 item: Stück
7 prospector: Goldsucher
8 loss: Verlust
9 adventurer: Abenteurer

Mr Woodland goes on and on. He talks about his company until the journalists are all tired and cold. The sun sets behind the mountains. It's getting dark.
Peter yawns[1]. "I really hope that Mr Woodland finishes his speech soon! I'm so tired and we have quite a long day ahead of us."
Justus looks at the evening sky. "We sure do! Tomorrow our big adventure is going to start!"

The next morning everybody in Dawson is outside, waiting for the race to start. The Main Street is crowded[2]. People cheer[3]. A band plays songs. Dogs are barking and jumping. Mushers and their assistants try to calm them down[4]. Everywhere reporters try to take photographs or get interviews. Carol has a TV camera on her shoulder, while Peter and Bob put their luggage[5] on one of their ski-doos.
Meanwhile, Justus watches Francis and her dogs.
"Sit down, Fjell!" she shouts. "Good dog! Be nice, Thunder!"
Behind her, another woman checks her sled. She is much taller than Francis and has long blond hair.
"I guess that this lady is Candace Duskin." Slowly, Justus walks over to his two friends.
"A masterpiece of deduction[6]!" Peter laughs. "There are only two women in this race. But let me show you what I can do!" He touches his forehead and looks as if he has to concentrate. "Well, well... that man on the left happens to be ... Gordon Hoke, and the man on the right is Jared Fox!"

1 to yawn: gähnen
2 crowded – full of people
3 to cheer: jubeln
4 to calm somebody down: jemanden beruhigen
5 luggage: Gepäck
6 deduction: Schlussfolgerung

"How do you know that?" Justus asks. He looks at Jared Fox, a thin man. He is pale[1] and seems[2] unhappy.
"I'm psychic[3]!" Peter smiles. "It's a gift that only works on very cold days."
"Yeah, right..." Justus says. "Come on, Peter. Tell me how you know all the names!"
"Magic!" Peter puts his sleeping bag on his ski-doo.
"Here!" Bob hands Justus a piece of paper. "That's how Peter does his magic: Carol just gave us a list with the names and the numbers of the mushers. Jared Fox is number three. You can see the number on his coat!"
"Bob! You ruined[4] my joke!" Peter complains[5]. He looks embarrassed[6].
Justus takes a look at the list. He reads the names of the mushers:

Number	Name
1	Hoke, Gordon
2	Moylan, Curtis
3	Fox, Jared
4	Duskin, Candace Jane
5	Norsworthy, Baxter
6	Studstill, Francis

"We should keep that!", he says. "It's good to have a list of all the people who might be saboteurs!"

1 pale: blass
2 to seem: scheinen
3 to be psychic: übersinnliche Fähigkeiten haben
4 to ruin: ruinieren, verderben
5 to complain: sich beschweren
6 to look embarrassed: verlegen aussehen

"I wonder where Baxter Norsworthy is!" Bob looks around.
"The man who thinks he is the greatest musher of all time?" Peter asks. He looks around too.
"Exactly, Mr Psychic," says Bob. He steps on a box to have a better view. "I think I see him! He is number five. It's that man over there. The guy with the black coat and the black sled."
"He doesn't look nice," Peter says. He wants to say something more but right in front of them Candace Duskin's dogs start to run. But it's not her turn to leave now. She shouts at her animals and tries to stop them. As hard as possible, she hits the brakes[1].
"Go back to your little Barbie castle, Baby!" Baxter Norsworthy shouts.
"You wish[2], Baxter! I'll win this race, you'll see!" Candace Duskin shouts back at him. "I'll be in Fairbanks first!"
"You will not!" Baxter Norsworthy puts a blue box on top of his sled.
"Now starting: Jared Fox!" a voice from the loudspeakers says.
Fox's dogs pull the sled onto the snowy street. At a speed of[3] nearly thirty miles per hour they race away.
"What a great departure[4]!" the loudspeaker shouts. After that, the next numbers are called and the other mushers drive away. The crowd cheers.
Francis is the last of them. She seems to be nervous but she smiles. Justus waves[5] his hand as she drives by. "Good luck, Francis!"
"Let's follow her!" Carol shouts. The reporter jumps onto her ski-doo. "Hurry up, boys! We have to follow the mushers!"

1 to hit the brakes: auf die Bremse treten, bremsen
2 you wish: das hättest du wohl gerne! *(umgangssprachlich)*
3 at a speed of: mit einer Geschwindigkeit von
4 departure – *hier:* Abfahrt
5 to wave: winken

The next moment, The Three Investigators drive out into the cold wilderness.

Detective Question 3

Why does Justus want to keep a list of all the mushers?

4. Wilderness

TR. 04

After two hours they take a short break[1]. Their arms and legs hurt. It's not easy to ride on the ski-doos and it's very cold. Around them there is nothing but trees, rocks and snow. A fierce[2] wind is blowing. Bob touches his lips. They are sore[3]. Nevertheless[4] he is enjoying the ride. He has already seen a moose[5] and a white jackrabbit[6]. Peter runs in a little circle to get warm again. "One hour more on the ski-doo and I will freeze!"

But Peter doesn't freeze. They drive for several hours. In the afternoon they meet the musher Gordon Hoke. He is a man with grey hair and a nice smile. Carol films his sled. Later they also meet Jared Fox. He still looks pale and unhappy. His dogs are having a hard time[7] going up a hill.
"Go Runner! Go Kid!" Fox shouts at his dogs. "Do not let me down!"
"He seems desperate[8]!" Justus says.
"It looks like he is going to cry!" Peter adds. "I think he is afraid of goblins and monsters!"
"Goblins!" Carol laughs. "I would like to film some goblins!"
"I hope we do not meet any," The Second Investigator says. "Goblins, witches and monsters should better stay at home when I'm out here!"

1 to take a break: eine Pause machen
2 fierce – *hier:* scharf
3 sore: wund, schmerzhaft
4 nevertheless: trotzdem
5 moose: Elch
6 jackrabbit: Hase
7 to have a hard time: es schwer haben, Probleme haben
8 desperate: verzweifelt

Jared Fox is just driving away when they spot[1] a blue ski-doo. Somebody is driving towards them. It's a good-looking man in his mid thirties.
"You seem to be in a rush[2]!" Carol says to him. She smiles.
"I missed the start of the race because my alarm clock is broken," the man explains.
"Are you a journalist too?" Carol asks.
"I'm a photographer," the man says and points to a brand new camera. "My name is Duane Carpenter. I come from Anchorage."
"Pleased to meet you, Mr Carpenter! I'm Carol Ford, a reporter from Southern California," Carol introduces[3] herself and the boys.
"We could travel together," Duane Carpenter says. "It's much safer to stay together than to drive through this forest alone. A lot of bad things can happen here."
Carol agrees with him enthusiastically[4]. Obviously[5] she likes Duane Carpenter. The boys look at each other and smile.

At nine o'clock in the evening the small group meets Baxter Norsworthy. The man with the black coat and the wild black hair camps near the trail. Across the next hill they also find Francis and her dogs. The young woman is feeding her dogs.
Bob looks at the food. It smells nasty[6] but the dogs like it.
"My dogs need hot meat and fish!" Francis explains. "Also, I have to cover them in blankets[7] and check their paws[8]."
"Is everything all right?" Justus asks.

1 to spot: bemerken
2 to be in a rush: in Eile sein
3 to introduce someone: jemanden vorstellen
4 enthusiastic: enthusiastisch
5 obviously: offensichtlich
6 nasty – *hier*: eklig
7 blanket: Decke
8 paw: Pfote

"Yes!" Francis answers. "The dogs are healthy and the weather is fine."

"No signs of sabotage?" Justus whispers.

"No! And why are you whispering?" Francis asks.

"I am whispering because I do not want anybody to listen to our conversation. Who knows, maybe the saboteur is close! Everybody is suspicious[1]!"

"Poor Spooky!" Francis pats her dog. He wags his tail. "You're a suspect[2]!"

The dog licks her hand. "Have you seen this? This is suspicious behavior!" Francis laughs.

"You are making fun of me!" Justus doesn't laugh. "But this is serious[3]! Sabotage can be very dangerous!"

"I know that!" Francis opens her tent. "But lack of[4] sleep is also very dangerous! We can talk tomorrow, okay? Right now, I'm too tired to think about sabotage or anything else. Good night."

Carol, Duane Carpenter and The Three Investigators decide to camp close to Francis. While Justus tries to light a fire[5], Bob looks at the dark forest. Something is moving between the trees. Francis' dogs howl. Bob gets goosebumps[6]. "It might be a bear!" he says to Peter.

"I don't think so!" says Duane Carpenter. "Bears usually sleep through the winter. They only come out a few times. And then they are very slow and tired."

1 suspicious: verdächtig
2 a suspect: ein Verdächtiger
3 serious: ernst
4 lack of: Mangel an
5 to light a fire: ein Feuer anzünden
6 goosebumps: Gänsehaut

Again, Bob looks into the darkness. Something is out there! But what? A pair of eyes gleam[1] in the dark. Then they vanish[2]. Bob and Peter stare into the darkness. After a while Bob turns to Justus. "Have you seen something, Just?"

"How? Can't you see that I'm busy[3] with the fire? It's hard to light one when your hands are frozen!" He throws away the match[4]. "It doesn't work!" Justus lights another match but it falls out of his stiff fingers. He curses[5] the cold weather.

"I heard that, Justus!" Carol looks out of the tent. "That's enough swearing[6]!"

"I'm sorry!" Again Justus reaches for[7] a match. Bob smiles and hands his friend a plastic bottle. "Here, try the chemical fire-starter."

Finally Justus manages to light the fire. They boil[8] water and prepare[9] their dinner.

After a snack of dry caribou-meat[10], energy-bars and bread they creep into the tent. Bob wraps himself up[11] in his sleeping bag. He shudders[12]. "I'm so cold! I'm afraid I'll never feel warm again!"

"I would give anything for a hot shower!" Peter adds.

"Maybe you can have one tomorrow!" Justus tells his friend. "We're going to the small town Beaver Falls. It's a checkpoint where veterinarians[13] check the dogs. Also the mushers get food and a place to sleep. I think they also have bathrooms at the checkpoint."

1 to gleam: leuchten
2 to vanish: verschwinden
3 busy with: beschäftigt mit
4 match: Streichholz
5 to curse something: etwas verfluchen
6 to swear: fluchen
7 to reach for something: nach etwas greifen
8 to boil: kochen
9 to prepare dinner: das Abendessen zubereiten
10 caribou meat: Karibufleisch (Karibus sind nordamerikanische Rentiere)
11 he wraps himself up: er wickelt sich ein
12 to shudder: schaudern, zittern
13 veterinarian: Tierarzt

"I hope so!" Bob says. "I can't wait until tomorrow!"
"Good night!" Peter mumbles.
Outside the tent a dog barks. An owl[1] cries. The wind howls[2]. Snow is falling. It's cold and also a little bit spooky[3], but finally Peter and his friends manage to[4] sleep.

Detective Question 4

How do The Three Investigators know that Carol finds Duane Carpenter attractive?

1 owl: Eule
2 to howl: heulen
3 spooky: gruselig
4 to manage to sleep: es schaffen, zu schlafen

5. Bad Signs!

TR. 05

When Justus wakes his friends they are still very tired.
"I haven't slept enough!" Peter says and rubs his face.
"But you have to get up!" Justus tells him. "Francis and her dogs are already gone! Mushers don't sleep very long when they take part[1] in a race. Sometimes they only sleep for three or four hours!"
The boys put their shoes on and climb out of the tent. It's still dark and also very cold.
"I want to go back into the tent!" Bob says. He stretches his arms.
"Then you will miss this!" Duane Carpenter points to the sky.
Above them green and red lights dance.
"Northern lights!" Peter looks at the colours that stretch from the mountaintops[2] up to the stars.
"Aurora borealis!" Justus explains to his friends. "It happens when electrons collide[3] with atoms of the upper atmosphere of the earth. Some ancient[4] cultures thought that the lights were a sign[5] from the gods. For example a sign of war or danger."
"No matter what they are, they look beautiful to me!" Bob says.
Peter looks at his friends. "I hope that this is not a message from the gods telling us that we are in danger! The green lights look nice but I do not like the red ones!"
"Well I like them all!" Duane Carpenter takes a picture with his camera. "This is wonderful!"
"But that picture will be blurred[6], Duane!" Carol tells him. "It's too dark to take photographs without a tripod[7]."

1 to take part in: teilnehmen an
2 mountaintops: Berggipfel
3 to collide: zusammenprallen
4 ancient cultures: antike Kulturen
5 sign: Zeichen
6 blurred: verschwommen, unscharf
7 tripod: Stativ

"No, it's okay that way, Carol. This camera is very good. It's brand new! I never blur pictures[1] with it."
"Really?" Carol looks surprised. She wants to say something but she stops because they hear a howl. It comes out of the dark forest.
"Ouuuuuuuuuuuuuuuuuuuuu!"
"Is it a dog?" Bob asks.
"I don't know," Justus answers. He stares into the darkness between the trees.
"It might be wolves," says Duane Carpenter.
"Do they attack humans?" Peter doesn't like the situation.
"Usually they don't," Justus explains. "But that doesn't mean that they're not dangerous – especially when there are a lot of them out there. And ..." As fast as possible, Justus jumps out of the way because all of a sudden a sled appears[2] on the trail. It's Baxter Norsworthy.
"Watch out!" Justus shouts, as the musher drives by.
"He nearly collided with us!" Carol says. "He should be more careful!"
"He wants to win and doesn't care about anything else," says Bob.
Meanwhile, Peter tries to roll up his sleeping bag. The sleeping bag seems to have a mind of its own[3]. "I hate this!" Peter shouts. "Wolves and nasty sleeping bags are most definitely[4] the two things I can really do without[5]!"

"He is so suspicious!" Peter climbs off his ski-doo. It's early afternoon and the group is having a short break. Finally the sun comes out and it warms up a little.
"Who?" Bob asks. He drinks hot tea from a metal mug.

1 to blur pictures: unscharfe Fotos machen
2 to appear: erscheinen
3 to have a mind of one's own: seinen eigenen Kopf haben
4 most definitely: ganz bestimmt
5 to do without something: ohne etwas auskommen

"Baxter Norsworthy!" Peter answers. "He is a bad man! Look what happened this morning! He doesn't care if somebody gets hurt. He just wants to win this race!"

"They all want to win this race!" Justus eats a piece of bread with cheese on it. "We don't have just one suspicious musher, but six! Remember that!"

"And how are we going to find out who is doing the sabotage? I mean, if there **is** a saboteur?" Peter also takes a piece of bread.

"We will watch them tonight! All the mushers have to stop at Beaver Falls. They have to stay there for some hours. That is our chance to investigate!" Justus wants to say more, but a snowball hits him.

"Peter!" he shouts. "Stop that! Don't shoot at me!"

"Well," Peter smiles and turns to the Third Investigator. "I think you're right. I should throw a snowball at Bob."

"Stop!" Bob wants to put down his mug. But it's too late. The ball hits his arm. Bob's tea splashes[1] everywhere. "Well done!" the Third Investigator says sarcastically. "Why did you do that?"

"Because yesterday, you ruined my joke and told Justus about the list with all the mushers. Also you told him that I'm not psychic and ..."

"A sled!" Justus interrupts[2] his friend. "A musher is coming!"

Justus is right. It's Candace Duskin.

"Hi there!" Candace greets the boys when she arrives. The dogs slow down and then stop.

"Today I wish I had a ski-doo," Candace Duskin tells them. Her voice is rough[3]. "My dogs are tired. I hope the veterinarians don't take some of them out of the race!"

"Does that happen sometimes?" Bob asks.

"The veterinarians are strict. The dogs have to be healthy and fit. Otherwise they are not allowed to run."

1 to splash everywhere: überall hin spritzen
2 to interrupt: unterbrechen
3 rough: rau, heiser

"Then good luck with the vets[1]!" Bob smiles.
"Thank you!" Candace Duskin throws her long blond hair over her shoulder. "I'm afraid I have to go now. I just met Francis and Jared. We talked a little and fed our dogs. Now I really have to hurry[2]!"
She jumps onto her sled. "See you in Beaver Falls, boys!"
The Three Investigators watch her drive into the snowy forest.
"She could be the saboteur too!" Justus says to his friends.
"Candace Duskin?" Peter shakes his head. "Not her! She is nice and pretty!"
"That's not an alibi, Peter!" Justus says. "Criminals can be pretty and they can pretend[3] to be nice!"
Peter takes another piece of bread. "Okay, you're right. But I still think that we have to watch Baxter Norsworthy. Something is not right about him! You will see!"

Detective Question 5

What is wrong with the way Peter decides who is suspicious and who is not suspicious?

1 vet: short for veterinarian
2 to hurry: sich beeilen
3 to pretend: so tun als ob

6. Arctic Autumn

TR. 06

Beaver Falls is a small town in the middle of nowhere. All 120 inhabitants[1] have gathered[2] at the town center to greet the mushers. There are tables with free food and drinks for everyone.

"We are happy the "Nordic Wilderness Race" also comes to our little town!" an old man tells Carol in an interview. "Of course we have our own events[3]! Each May we celebrate the "Day of the Beaver" and in September we have our bowling cup! Beaver Falls has its own bowling center! Do you want to see it?"

"Maybe later!" Carol Ford tries to smile. Then she turns to the boys. "Could you please bring all our things to the camp[4]?"

The boys nod. They drive towards a couple of cabins near the forest. In front of them a plastic beaver holds up a sign that says: "Camp 1 and 2".

The Three Investigators park their ski-doo and carry the sleeping bags into one cabin. Then they walk through the camp.

"Oh no!" Peter comes out of the restroom cabin. "There are no showers and there's only one sink[5]." Peter looks disappointed[6]. "And on top of that[7] the water is cold!"

Bob sighs. "Well, I guess that is just what life in the wilderness is like[8]!"

1 inhabitant: Einwohner, Bewohner
2 to gather: sammeln, *hier*: (sich) versammeln
3 event: Veranstaltung, Ereignis
4 camp: Lager
5 sink: Waschbecken
6 disappointed: enttäuscht
7 and on top of that: und obendrein
8 what something is like: wie etwas ist

In the first cabin, the boys meet Baxter Norsworthy and Gordon Hoke. The musher Curtis Moylan is with them. He is a tall man with a red face.
The room is warm. The men have lit a fire in a stove[1] and are drying their wet socks. There are little pools[2] of water on the floor.
"It's sad that you are ill. We will miss you!" Gordon Hoke says to Curtis Moylan. "What are you going to do now?"
Curtis Moylan sighs, "Tomorrow I will go back to Dawson on a small plane. I really have to see a doctor. I feel terrible. It could be a fever."
"The fewer mushers, the better!" Baxter Norsworthy sits down on a mat[3]. "Well, well: It's my lucky week! First, two mushers get ill in Dawson and now this ... Curtis gets ill too! But please don't come near me, Curtis. I don't want to catch[4] whatever you have!"
"Baxter!" Gordon Hoke says angrily. "This is not fair!"
"Let him talk!" says Moylan. "There's simply not enough room for Baxter's self-confidence[5] in this cabin."
"And no room for his terrible smell!" adds Gordon Hoke. "Baxter, you smell like a wet dog! You should go to the restrooms and wash yourself!"
Baxter Norsworthy smiles, then he opens his bag. "I don't need to wash myself!" He holds up a bottle of antiperspirant[6]. "This is "Arctic Autumn"! It smells just like the wilderness!" He sprays the antiperspirant on himself.
Peter coughs and Justus whispers: "I think you can kill bears with "Arctic Autumn"!"

1 stove: Ofen
2 pool – hier: Pfütze
3 mat: Matte, Matratze
4 to catch – *hier:* bekommen, angesteckt werden
5 self-confidence: Selbstbewusstsein
6 antiperspirant: Deodorant

The Second Investigator smiles. "I'm sure you can! That stuff is terrible!"
Baxter Norsworthy takes his blue box and creeps into his sleeping bag. "I'm going to sleep now, guys! So don't dare to disturb[1] me! Or better: Get out of the room and leave me alone!"
"Well, Baxter has never been polite to anyone," Curtis Moylan tells the boys. "I hope he gets disqualified[2]. Sometimes, he lets his dogs run without a break."
"That shouldn't happen!" Gordon Hoke says. "A musher has to care for his dogs."
"When the vets decide that mushers don't treat their dogs well enough, they have to quit[3] the race. They are very strict." Curtis Moylan looks out of the window. Outside the veterinarians are checking Candace Duskin's dogs. The young woman with the long blond hair stands next to her sled. She has pieces of ice in her hair and she looks very tired.

Thirty minutes later, the other woman, Francis, arrives at Beaver Falls. The Three Investigators meet her in front of the cabins.
"What a day!" Francis sighs. "The vets decided[4] that Spooky can't run any longer. He seems to be sick!"
"Maybe his paws hurt!" says Peter.
"No, the paws are okay. The vet said that he's got a stomach ache[5]!" She pats Spooky. "He ate a lot of meat this afternoon."
"Maybe someone put poison in his food!" Justus mumbles.
"He's one of my best dogs." Francis looks at the boys. "This is bad for me. And of course bad for poor Spooky."

1 to dare to disturb someone: es wagen, jemanden zu stören
2 disqualified: disqualifiziert
3 to quit: aufhören mit
4 to decide: beschließen
5 stomach ache: Bauchschmerzen

"Is that dog sick?" Two men in orange coats walk towards Francis. One of them is holding a bottle of beer in his hand.
"For a couple of dollars I will care for your dogs!" the man with the beer says. He can't walk straight.
"I certainly do not need your help!" Francis says. One of her dogs growls[1].
"Bad, bad doggie!" The man sips his beer. "Shut up[2] doggie!"
Candace Duskin steps out of one of the cabins. "Dogs do not like drunken people," she tells the two men. "So stay away from them!"
"Ok, we'll stay away! But if you need help, you can ask us. We work at the gas station[3]! It's only a third of a mile away from here, near the town center." Then the two men walk away.

Detective Question 6

In this chapter, there are two more signs that there may be a saboteur. What are they?

1 growl: knurren
2 shut up: sei still, halt's Maul *(umgangssprachlich)*
3 gas station: Tankstelle

7. A Trail[1] of Blood!

TR. 07

At eleven o'clock the camp is silent. But Peter can't sleep. From his mat he watches Baxter Norsworthy. The musher gets up and puts on his coat. The Second Investigator smells his antiperspirant "Arctic Autumn". It's still very strong. Norsworthy takes his sleeping bag and his blue box, then he leaves the cabin. When he opens the door, a cold wind blows into the room.

"We have to close the fridge or something terrible will happen!" Justus mumbles in his sleep. Peter smiles. Then he looks around. Everybody is asleep. Bob is lying next to him. Carol and Francis are sleeping in the left corner and Curtis Moylan and Duane Carpenter in the right corner. Candace Duskin, Gordon Hoke and Jared Fox are not in the room. Peter guesses[2] that they are sleeping in one of the other cabins.

The Second Investigator wants to watch Norsworthy. But Peter can't find his coat. He looks everywhere: In his bag, on the floor and inside his sleeping bag. After five minutes he finds out that Justus is using it as a pillow. Peter has to take Bob's coat instead[3]. As fast as possible, he puts it on. It's too short for him.

The night wind is very cold. Peter is sorry that he didn't take his scarf. In the distance, he hears music. The inhabitants of Beaver Falls are still celebrating. The Second Investigator sneaks[4] across the snowy yard[5]. He hears a cough. Baxter Norsworthy is close! Carefully Peter looks around the corner of the cabin. In the moonlight he sees the

1 trail: Spur
2 to guess – *hier*: vermuten
3 instead: statt dessen
4 to sneak: schleichen
5 yard – *hier*: Lagerplatz

musher and his dogs. Norsworthy steps onto his sled. "Go dogs, go!" he shouts.

Peter watches him drive away. "Too bad!" he whispers. "If Norsworthy has sabotaged one of the sleds, I have missed it! Just because Justus is sleeping on my jacket!" Peter walks towards the sleds. They stand in a dark corner behind the cabins. Peter can't see much. "Everything seems to be okay," he says to himself. Then he decides to go to the dogs. The animals sleep in a big blue tent. It's even darker than the corner with the sleds. Peter reaches into his pockets. He finds Bob's little flashlight[1]. His fingers are cold and stiff. But finally he manages to turn the flashlight on. The eyes of the dogs reflect[2] the light. Two dogs start to bark.

"Hush[3]!" Peter whispers. Then he looks around. Again, everything seems okay. He walks back to the cabin. On his way he points the flashlight at the snow. There are footprints[4] of mushers and dogs on the ground. All of a sudden[5] he stops. Peter feels goosebumps on his arms. He shivers[6]. There are dark stains[7] on the white snow. It's blood!

"Blood?" Justus is excited. Peter has gone back to the cabin and has woken up his friends.

"Why are you wearing my coat?" Bob asks.

"I'll tell you later!" Peter whispers. "Baxter Norsworthy has gone and I found a trail of blood!"

They run outside and Peter shows them the blood.

Justus turns on his flashlight. "There are footsteps in the snow!"

1 flashlight: Taschenlampe
2 to reflect: reflektieren, wiederspiegeln
3 Hush!: Psst!
4 footprints: Fuβspuren
5 all of a sudden – suddenly
6 to shiver: schaudern, zittern
7 stain: Fleck

"Have you seen somebody with a wound[1]?" Bob asks.
"No! If I had, I would have told you[2]!" Peter answers.
Justus slowly follows the trail of blood. "It leads right into the forest!"
"What if the saboteur is still out here?" Bob whispers. He feels his heart beat in his chest[3]. It's dangerous to go into the forest at night!
"No, it's not dangerous now. I'm sure the saboteur is Baxter Norsworthy!" Peter says as he walks through the deep snow. "And he isn't here anymore. The saboteur is gone and so is the danger."
"But there could be a wild animal that attacks[4] people. A bear or a wolf! Maybe it wasn't Mr Norsworthy, but an animal that attacked a musher!" Again Bob looks at the blood.
"You mean a wild animal came to the camp and attacked a person?" Peter feels uncomfortable[5]. "I don't like the idea!"
"There are no animal footprints around here." Justus' flashlight shines at some trees and bushes. They look spooky. Peter and Bob shiver.
"There!" All of a sudden, Justus stops.
"What?" Pete asks.
Justus doesn't answer. He runs towards a tree. "Miss Duskin!"
Now Bob and Peter also see the pretty young woman. She sits in front of a tree. Under the hood[6] of her coat they can see her bloodstained[7] forehead[8]. Her eyes are closed.

1 wound: Wunde
2 I would have told you: ich hätte dir Bescheid gesagt
3 chest: Brustkorb
4 to attack: angreifen
5 to feel uncomfortable: sich unwohl fühlen
6 hood: Kapuze
7 bloodstained: blutbefleckt
8 forehead: Stirn

"Come on, help me!" Justus tries to lift the woman. "I think she is unconscious[1]!"
"Let me do that!" Peter says. He is the strongest of The Three Investigators but even for him it's not easy to carry Candace Duskin. "Bob, you should run and call a doctor!" Peter says, out of breath[2], when they reach the edge of the forest.

"How do you feel?" The doctor looks at Candace Duskin's forehead.
"My head aches!" the blond woman answers. "And I feel a little bit dizzy[3]." She is very pale.
"What happened?" Justus asks her.
Candace Duskin doesn't answer right away. She looks out of the window. "I ... I do not know! I ..."
"Try to remember!" the photographer, Duane Carpenter says. "Did you go to your sled?"
"Yes! I think I wanted to go to my sled. I wanted to fetch[4] my sleeping bag." Candace Duskin touches her head.
"Do not do that!" the Doctor said. He places a band-aid[5] on the wound.
"And what happened when you reached the sleds?" Duane Carpenter asks. He looks excited.
"I heard something. But I thought it was just a dog. So I didn't stop. I walked over to my sled. Yes, that is what happened. Then, all of a sudden, I heard something behind me. But when I turned around something hard hit me over the head."

1 unconscious: bewusstlos
2 out of breath: außer Atem
3 I feel dizzy: mir ist schwindelig
4 to fetch: holen
5 band-aid: Pflaster

A tear runs down her pale cheek. "I don't want to give up now! The race is so important for me! Please let me go, Doctor! Please!"
"I think you will be okay tomorrow, Miss!" the doctor says. He puts another band-aid on her forehead. Then he looks at her. "Now, all you need is some sleep."

Detective Question 7

Which three mushers had the chance to hit Candace Duskin over the head?

8. Investigation

TR. 08

The next morning, The Three Investigators drive to the gas station in Beaver Falls. They need fuel[1] for their ski-doos. The men in the orange coats aren't there. A pretty girl with long brown hair stands behind the counter. Peter pays for the fuel and buys three cokes for himself and his friends. Together, the boys walk out into the sun. The morning is cold but beautiful. From the gas station they can see the forest and the mountains.

"I still wonder[2] what happened yesterday!" Justus opens his coke.

"Well, I think I know what happened: Baxter Norsworthy sees Candace Duskin, hits her and drives away!" Peter says. "And you know what: I also think that he has a weapon[3] in his blue box."

"Or maybe something to sabotage the sleds!" Bob adds. " He always takes the box with him, even when he sleeps. It's important to him!"

"Maybe he has poison in his box! He uses it to poison the dogs – like Spooky!" Peter says. "It could also be something to make people ill."

"I don't know. But what I know is that he didn't poison Spooky!" Justus answers. "Yesterday, he was not there when Francis fed her dogs. Remember that he is faster than the other mushers. He didn't stop with them. That is why he arrived at Beaver Falls first."

Justus takes the list out of his pocket, then he writes on the paper:

1 fuel: Benzin
2 to wonder – *hier:* sich fragen
3 weapon: Waffe

Number	Name
1	Hoke, Gordon – suspicious
2	~~Moylan, Curtis~~ – has to give up because he is ill
3	Fox, Jared – suspicious!
4	Duskin, Candace Jane – victim[1] in Beaver Falls
5	Norsworthy, Baxter – suspicious!
6	Studstill, Francis – asleep while Candace is attacked

"Of course it can't be Francis," Peter looks at the list. "She slept in our cabin when Miss Duskin was attacked."

"Well, she could have asked somebody else to do it," Justus says. "Maybe someone from Beaver Falls. The drunken men for example!"

"How about Duane Carpenter!" Bob takes the list and writes his name down.

"Why?" Peter looks at his friend. "Duane Carpenter is a photographer, not a musher. He doesn't even take part in the race!"

"Peter is right. Besides, Mr Carpenter was in the cabin yesterday. He has an alibi too," Justus answers.

"But when we came back with Candace Duskin he was so excited." Bob sips his coke. "Moreover[2], I don't think he's a real photographer!"

"Not a photographer? Why?" Peter asks.

"Because he lied to us[3]! He said that he has a professional camera that can take pictures in the dark. That's not true! I know a lot about cameras and he just has a normal one. Without a tripod his night-pictures will be blurred!"

"We should check his identity!" Justus says.

"But how?" Peter asks. "We do not have internet access[4] here in Beaver Falls!"

1 victim: Opfer
2 moreover: außerdem
3 to lie to someone: jemanden anlügen
4 internet access: Internetzugang

"Let's call Jelena in Rocky Beach!" Bob says. Jelena is one of his friends. She's very clever.
"I don't like Jelena," Justus growls.
"But she has helped us before, don't you remember?" Bob says. "There's a phone booth[1] next to the gas station!"
"Okay, then go and call her," Justus sighs. "Please ask her to check the mushers as well. I want to know all about them! And tell her that we are going to call her back as soon as possible. Maybe tomorrow or the day after tomorrow."

Detective Question 8

How does Bob know that Duane Carpenter is not a real photographer?
Bonus question: What do you think is in Baxter Norsworthy's blue box? (Diese Frage wird im Text bisher nicht beantwortet, also kannst du deiner Phantasie freien Lauf lassen.)

1 phone booth: Telefonzelle

9. The River

TR. 09

It's already late in the afternoon when Carol and the boys stop for a break. This time Duane Carpenter is not with them. He wants to go with Baxter Norsworthy to take some photographs of him and his dogs. Carol films a frozen waterfall and the snow-covered mountains.
"Today the mushers have to cross the Yukon River!" Carol tells the boys. "It's a very dangerous trip, because there are cracks[1] in the ice!"
"I have heard about that!" Justus says. "The people from the race place[2] trail signs[3] at the river. They show the mushers where it's safe to cross the ice."
"We should camp here!" Carol decides. "The Yukon River is just one mile away and I want to film Francis when she crosses the river."
"I'm going to gather some wood for the fire!" Peter says. He takes an axe and walks towards a group of trees. After a couple of minutes he hears the sound of a ski-doo. Peter looks around. The sun is just setting and it's already dark in the forest. Somewhere among the trees Peter sees something orange!
"It could be the men from Beaver Falls!" he whispers to himself. "They had orange coats! But what are they doing here near the Yukon River?"
Peter takes the wood and walks back to Carol and his friends. He tells them about the men on the ski-doo.
"Are you sure that you saw the men from Beaver Falls?" Justus asks.
"Yes!" Peter answers. "I saw the orange coats."
"Maybe they were checking the trail signs!" Bob says.

1 crack: Sprung, Riss
2 to place: platzieren
3 trail signs: Wegweiser

"Or maybe they were doing something else," Justus answers. "We do not know much about those men, but they could be involved[1] in the sabotage!"
Peter and Bob take the wood and light a fire. All of a sudden Carol shouts: "Look, there are Gordon Hoke and Baxter Norsworthy!"
The two mushers pass the camp. Gordon Hoke greets them but Baxter Norsworthy doesn't.
"I will wait for Francis!" Carol says. "I don't want to film Baxter Norsworthy. I really don't like him."

They wait for a long time. A full moon rises above the dark trees. The snow sparkles[2]. The boys sit around the fire. "Francis is late!" Bob says.
"I hope she is well[3]!" Carol adds.
Finally, they hear a dog bark. "It must be Francis!" Justus gets up. "Yes! There's a light!"
"Hurry up!" Carol jumps towards her ski-doo. "I want to film her! Peter, can you drive my ski-doo and take me to the Yukon River?"
"What can we do?" Justus asks.
"Stay here and watch the camp. Peter and I will be back soon!" Carol shouts. She puts the camera on her shoulder. Justus hands her the camera bag.
Then Peter steps on the gas[4]. The ski-doo races across the snow. "Drive as fast as possible!" Carol shouts.
Again there are northern lights in the sky. Red and green lines of light dance in the cold air. "Bad signs!" Peter mumbles.

1 to be involved – *hier*: beteiligt sein
2 to sparkle: glitzern
3 she is well: es geht ihr gut
4 to step on the gas: auf das Gaspedal treten, Gas geben

He stops at the top of a hill and looks down at the river. "The ice!" Peter gasps[1]. The Yukon River is still frozen but there are black cracks on the ice! "The ice is breaking!" Peter shouts.

"What?" Carol shouts back. Now she also sees the dangerous cracks.

"We have to warn Francis!" Again Peter steps on the gas.

At the same moment, Francis and her dogs appear at the top of another hill. Peter sees that something isn't right! The sled isn't going in a straight line. The dogs are out of control[2]! Peter is alarmed[3]. Maybe Francis is unconscious! The sled is going down the hill at high speed. It's much too fast!

"Stop!" Peter shouts. But Francis doesn't stop at the river.

"Don't cross the ice!" Peter shouts. No reaction!

The sled reaches[4] the Yukon River and the dogs run out onto the ice.

Detective Question 9

Why does Peter think the men he sees at the Yukon River are the men from Beaver Falls? Do you think he is right?

1 to gasp: nach Luft schnappen
2 out of control: außer Kontrolle
3 to be alarmed: erschrocken sein
4 to reach: erreichen

10. Danger!

TR. 10

"We have to stop her!" Peter drives down the hill towards the river.
"No, it's too dangerous!" Carol shouts. "The ski-doo is too heavy for the ice!"
"Then I have to run!" Peter jumps off the ski-doo. The Second Investigator is a fast runner but the dogs are very fast as well. They are running at full speed. When Peter steps onto the ice it makes terrible sounds! Peter hopes that it won't break. Nevertheless, he doesn't stop. He follows the sled. Now, it's just six yards[1] away! His lungs hurt but he keeps running. Just five yards! Peter tries to run faster. It's not easy to run on the ice. Peter slides[2] and nearly falls. Four yards to the sled! Three yards! Peter shouts, "Stop!" But again, Francis doesn't react[3]. The ice on Peter's left cracks. He can see the black water of the river. Two yards! There is a second crack on his right! He knows that he is in great danger. One crack more and Francis, the dogs and Peter could drown[4] in the Yukon River! One yard! Now Peter can reach the sled. He jumps onto it and steps on the brake. The dogs run to the left. The reins[5] stretch. The sled slides to the right and nearly tips over[6]. Peter falls onto the ice. Finally[7], after terrible seconds, the sled stops.

1 yard: Längeneinheit, 1 yard = ca. 91 cm
2 to slide: rutschen
3 to react: reagieren
4 to drown: ertrinken
5 reins: Zügel
6 to tip over: umkippen
7 finally: endlich

"Francis!" Peter gets up again. His legs hurt. Now he feels the cold. Slowly, he walks over to the musher. "Francis, wake up!" Peter pats her shoulder. Francis opens her eyes and looks at him. Then she says with a thin voice, "A burger menu and a coke, Miss!"

...

"I didn't drink enough water!" Francis says. Together with The Three Investigators and Carol she is sitting in front of a small fire.

"You could have died out there!" Carol hands her a mug with hot tea.

"Do you think Baxter Norsworthy and Gordon Hoke crossed the river at that place?" Bob asks.

"There are no sled-tracks on the Yukon River," Peter answers. "I think the other mushers saw the cracks in the ice. Then they searched for[1] a better place to cross the river."

"So, the trail signs are wrong?" Carol asks.

"Well, they didn't show the safest way!" Justus answers.

"Then the men in the orange coats were not checking them!" Bob says. "Maybe they even took them away and placed them at a dangerous place!"

"But why?" Peter asks.

"It's sabotage!" Justus answers. "When the trail signs are wrong the mushers have to stop and find a new way. So they lose time!"

"We have to warn the other mushers!" Bob says, when he spots a light near the forest. It's Candace Duskin, the blond woman. She stops when she sees them.

"It's good that you're stopping here!" Justus tells her. "The trail signs are wrong! You have to be very careful when you cross the river."

"Yes," Bob adds, "you should wait until tomorrow. It's much safer to go by daylight."

1 to search for: suchen (nach)

"I haven't got the time," Candace Duskin answers. "I have to find a better way across the ice. But I will be careful – I promise!" Then she drives away.

The musher Jared Fox arrives ten minutes later. He decides to stay with them until morning. "It's not safe to cross the river at night!" Jared Fox says. He and Francis feed their dogs. The animals are excited.

"What is wrong with you?" Jared Fox asks one of his dogs. "You are so nervous!"

"My dogs are nervous too!" Francis says. She pats them and talks to them. "Calm down!" But the dogs don't calm down. They bark and even growl! A cold wind blows. At the same moment, the small fire dies. Now, only a pale moon lights the camp.

"Something is wrong!" Francis says. She looks into the night.

"Yes, the dogs smell something!" Jared Fox adds nervously.

"What is it?" Peter asks. He doesn't get an answer.

The dogs start to whine[1]. They tuck their tails between their legs[2] – a sign that they are frightened. Also, the fur at their necks stands up.

"Danger!" Francis whispers.

Bob shivers. A cloud covers a big part of the moon. The Third Investigator rubs his glasses. He can't see properly[3]. Slowly the cloud moves across the sky. After two minutes, the moon comes out again. Bob looks north and gasps. He turns to his friends. "There's something moving over there!"

1 to whine: winseln
2 they tuck their tails between their legs: sie ziehen den Schwanz ein
3 properly: vernünftig, richtig

Now they all look at the edge[1] of the forest. Bob is right! Dark shadows are moving between the bushes. They hear the crackle[2] of twigs[3]. An owl flies up and cries. Slowly the shadows move forwards – towards[4] their camp!

Detective Question 10

How can you tell when dogs are scared, what do you think they are scared of?

1 edge: Rand
2 crackle: Knistern, Knacken
3 twig: Zweig
4 towards: auf.... zu

11. Justus, the Hero

TR. 11

"Wolves!" Jared Fox shouts.

"Wolves?" Peter looks angry. "This is a terrible night! First I nearly drown in the Yukon River and now I have to fight against wolves!"

"There are at least six or seven wolves!" Francis says. She seems frightened.

"We need fire!" Justus says.

"Why?" Bob asks.

"Because wolves are afraid of fire!" Justus shouts.

"Hurry up!" Francis runs to her sled. "I'll try to calm down my dogs."

"Where is the fire-starter?" Peter asks. He looks into his bag. There is no fire-starter.

"You used it an hour ago to light the fire," Bob says.

"But where is it now?" Peter is nervous. He looks into other bags.

"The wolves are coming!" Jared Fox points towards the forest. His dogs jump in fear. Jared Fox's sled tips over. "Hush! Stay calm, dogs!" he tells them.

"Do you have fire-starter, Sir?" Bob runs to Jared Fox's sled.

"Wait!" Jared Fox shouts. He turns around. "Take care of my dogs, boy! I'll search for the fire-starter!" He opens the big bag on his sled. "I'm sorry, but I don't want you to spill[1] my fire-starter. It's a dangerous chemical!"

"Here, Sir!" Justus hands the musher several long pieces of wood. "We can use them as torches[2]!"

Jared Fox takes the wood and sets it on fire[3].

Meanwhile, the wolves arrive at the camp. The boys can see their eyes. They reflect the red and yellow light of the fire.

1 to spill: verschütten
2 torch: Fackel
3 to set on fire: anzünden

A big grey wolf growls and shows his big teeth. The dogs whine again. "Go away!" Justus shouts and waves a burning piece of wood. Again, the wolf growls.
"They aren't afraid enough!" Peter shouts. The wolves come closer, and closer.
"Do something, Justus!" Bob says.
"Here, take the wood!" Justus hands the burning torch to Peter. Then he runs to his ski-doo. "I have an idea!"
"What are you doing?" Carol asks.
"I'll use this!" Justus returns with a flare gun[1]. "This is a special pistol that you can use to call for help. It shoots big glowing[2] balls into the air!"
"But there is nobody out there who can help us!" Bob says. "Besides, the help will be too late. We are in real danger now!"
"I don't want to shoot a ball into the air," Justus answers. "I want to shoot it right in front of the wolves!" Justus aims and shoots. The pistol fires with a "bang!". A red ball of light shoots out of it and hits the snow. The wolves jump and whine. Purple smoke[3] fills the air. Now the wolves are afraid. The smoke burns their eyes[4]. One of them howls. Then they run away.
Justus blows the smoke from his gun like a cowboy. He smiles. "Well, you should never mess with[5] Justus Jonas!"

Detective Question 11

Jared Fox does not want Peter to look for his fire starter. What reason does he give for this[6]?

1 flare gun: Leuchtpistole
2 glowing: leuchtend
3 purple smoke: violetter Rauch
4 burns their eyes: brennt in ihren Augen
5 to mess with someone: sich mit jemanden anlegen
6 to give a reason: einen Grund angeben

12. A Phone in Stone

TR. 12

"We should call Jelena! It's time we ask her what she found out!" Justus Jonas says when they arrive in Stone. Stone is a small town like Beaver Falls. The mushers have to stay here for at least ten hours. The Three Investigators park the ski-doos in front of the local school gym[1].

"That's our camp for tonight!" Bob tells them. "All the mushers stay here in the gym."

"But there is no phone around here!" Peter says.

They have to walk to the town center. Next to a little coffee-shop they find a phone booth. Bob puts some coins into the slot and dials[2] Jelena's number. After a short time Jelena answers the phone: "Jelena Charcova!"

"Hi, this is Bob!"

"Hello Bob! It's great that you are still alive and not frozen to death[3]!" Jelena laughs. Bob laughs too. Then he asks: "Did you find anything about Duane Carpenter on the internet?"

"No. There's no information about this photographer!" Jelena tells him. "I also called directory enquiries[4]. They don't have an entry[5] for a photographer called Duane Carpenter either. There is no Duane Carpenter in Anchorage."

"So he lied to us! He is not a photographer. Maybe "Duane Carpenter" is not even his real name!" Bob is excited. "And how about the others?"

"Well, I found something about Baxter Norsworthy on the internet. He's thirty-six years old. He's divorced and has a little daughter. Ten

1 gym: Turnhalle
2 to dial: wählen
3 frozen to death: erfroren
4 directory enquiries: Telefonauskunft
5 entry: Eintrag

years ago he was arrested[1] when he got into a fight with another man."

"He is rather aggressive!" Bob tells her. "The other mushers don't like him."

"There also was a short article about Gordon Hoke. He is Alaska's oldest musher. This is his last race. He retires[2] this year."

"And Jared Fox?" Bob asks.

Jelena laughs again. "Fox is called "The Monster Musher" or "The Fairy Tale[3] Man"! He said in an interview that he was followed by spooky creatures. He is a good musher but he's not very lucky. He lost a lot of the big races."

"Maybe he's trying to win this one by means of[4] sabotage!" Bob says.

"It's possible[5]!" Jelena answers. "Do you want to know something about Candace Jane Duskin?"

"Of course!"

"I found three articles about her. She has always been a winner. Miss Duskin is the daughter of a ranger[6]. She grew up in the wilderness between the Yukon River and a small town called Beaver Falls. Later, she won several beauty contests[7] and also starred in a TV series called "Mountain Girls"."

"Interesting!" Bob says. "You found out a lot, Jelena! That's great!"

"Oh, by the way: I also heard that Mr Woodland promised a five hundred dollar reward to any person who brings back his gold nugget!"

1 to be arrested: festgenommen werden
2 to retire: in Ruhestand gehen
3 fairy tale: Märchen
4 by means of: mittels
5 possible: möglich
6 ranger: Förster
7 beauty contest: Schönheitswettbewerb

"This man really loves his gold," Bob smiles. "And he's so into[1] the gold rush!"
"I know!" Jelena answers. "He has a private gold rush museum! When he was younger, Mr Woodland used to dig for gold in the mountains – just for fun. But some years ago he had an accident[2]. He hurt his leg. Since then he supports other adventurers."
"This is a lot of information!" Bob says. "Thank you so much!"
"You're welcome!" Jelena answers. "Maybe you could reward[3] me with a gift from Alaska! Something special[4]!"
"I'll get you a nice bear!" Bob promises.

Detective Question 12

Duane Carpenter is not who he says he is. Still, it is not likely[5] that he is the saboteur. Why?

1 to be into something: an etwas interessiert sein, sich für etwas begeistern
2 accident: Unfall
3 to reward someone: jemanden belohnen
4 special: besonders
5 likely: wahrscheinlich

13. The blue Box

TR. 13

"Baxter Norsworthy committed a crime?" Peter asks. The boys are sitting on the blue mats in the gym.

"Yes, but that was ten years ago!" Bob says.

"We should really take a look at his box. It's the most important clue[1] in this case!" Peter jumps up.

"I cannot come with you!" Bob says. "I just promised Carol to help her with an interview."

"But I'll go!" Justus gets up. "Right now, Baxter Norsworthy is taking a shower. That is the perfect chance to inspect[2] his blue box!"

Bob leaves the gym to help Carol. Peter and Justus walk into the men's changing room[3]. There are no people in the room. Baxter Norsworthy's bag is lying on the floor.

"Where's the blue box?" Peter asks.

"Under the bench[4]!" Justus answers. He kneels down[5].

"Hurry up! Open it!" Peter demands[6]. "I'm sure we'll find a clue that Norsworthy is the saboteur!"

"Or maybe we'll find the stolen gold and Jack London's bag!" Justus says.

"Or maybe you'll find something else!" an angry voice says. Drops[7] of water drip[8] down on the boys.

Alarmed, Justus and Peter turn around and look at Baxter Norsworthy!

1 clue: Anhaltspunkt
2 inspect: untersuchen
3 changing room: Umkleideraum
4 bench: Bank
5 to kneel down: niederknien, sich hinknien
6 to demand: verlangen
7 drops: Tropfen
8 to drip: tropfen

"What?" Bob shouts when Peter tells him what happened in the changing room. "I can't believe it!"

The three boys are sitting in a small coffee-shop near the gym.

"But it's true!" Peter smiles.

"It's so strange!" Bob stirs his hot chocolate. "He carries a stuffed toy[1] with him!"

"Yes! It's a pig! His daughter gave it to him. It's a talisman[2]."

"He was very angry that we opened his box. He didn't want anybody to see the toy," Justus tells Bob.

"Of course not!" Bob laughs.

"But he could still be the saboteur!" Peter says.

"I know what to do!" Justus shows his friend a bottle of "Arctic Autumn". "I bought this antiperspirant in the shop next door."

"Why? What are you going to do with it?" Peter asks.

Justus doesn't answer. Instead he sprays "Arctic Autumn" at Peter.

"Stop that!" Peter lifts[3] his hands. "It smells terrible!" He sniffs[4] his coat. "Now I smell like Baxter Norsworthy!"

"That's good! Now, get up. I can see Miss Duskin outside the coffee-shop. Please go out and talk to her. Then come back!"

Peter doesn't understand why he has to do this, but he gets up. He leaves the coffee-shop to talk to the blond woman.

After five minutes he returns[5] to their table.

"And, what did she say?" Justus asks.

"Candace Duskin said: "Peter! You smell terrible! What have you done? You should take a long shower!" Peter answers.

"That is exactly what I want to hear!" Justus says. "She can smell the antiperspirant! That means that it wasn't Baxter Norsworthy who hit her!"

1 stuffed toy: Stofftier
2 talisman: Talisman, Glücksbringer
3 to lift: heben
4 to sniff: schnüffeln, riechen
5 to return: zurückkommen

"I don't understand this theory!" Bob says.
"Well, Mr Norsworthy used "Arctic Autumn" the night somebody hit Candace Duskin."
"Yes, he smelled terrible. Like Peter does now!" Bob smiles. "But still I don't understand why this is an alibi for Baxter Norsworthy."
"Imagine the following situation: Baxter Norsworthy uses "Arctic Autumn" and goes out to his sled. He sees Candace Duskin and walks over to her[1]. What would happen?"
"She smells him?" Peter asks.
"Yes! Exactly! He smells so strong that Candace Duskin recognizes[2] him. But the night in Beaver Falls she didn't smell anything. So it wasn't Baxter Norsworthy who hit her!" Justus explains.
"So, somebody else hit her!"
"Yes! It was Jared Fox!" Justus says. "He doesn't have an alibi. And he doesn't want anybody to go near his sled. Do you remember last night, when you wanted to use his fire-starter?"
"Jared Fox is the saboteur?" Peter asks. "Are you sure?"
"No, Fox isn't the saboteur." Justus sips his hot chocolate. "But he wants to hide something!"
"The gold!" Bob whispers.
"Exactly! And Jack London's bag!" Justus adds.
"But who is the saboteur?" Bob asks.
"Candace Duskin is the saboteur!" Justus says.
"What?" Bob and Peter shout.
"In Beaver Falls, she wanted to break Baxter Norsworthy's sled. But it was standing next to Jared Fox's sled. Jared Fox saw her outside and thought that she wanted to steal the gold. He was frightened! So he hit her and ran away."

1 to walk over to someone: zu jemandem herübergehen
2 to recognize: erkennen

"That's right! Now it makes sense[1]!" Bob says. "But how can we prove[2] that she really is the saboteur?"
"Do you remember our special paste[3]?" Justus shows his friends a small green pot. He opens it. Inside, there is a paste that looks like glue[4]. "When somebody touches the paste, he gets black stains on his hands. And the paste does not wash off[5] for days! It's a special chemical mixture[6]."
"You are going to set a trap[7] for Candace Duskin!" Peter says.
"Yes! I'll smear[8] paste on Baxter Norsworthy's water bottle, his box and his sled."
"Why on Baxter Norsworthy's things?"
"He is the best musher in this race! He will win this race. Candace Duskin has to sabotage him as soon as possible. Tonight is the last chance for her! Tomorrow he is the first musher to start. Then he will be gone."
"We have to tell him!" Bob says.
"I'll go and talk to him," Justus gets up. "And then I'll smear the paste on his things!"

Detective Question 13

Why can't Baxter Norsworthy be the person who hit Candace Duskin over the head?

1 to make sense: Sinn machen
2 to prove: beweisen
3 special paste: spezielle Paste
4 glue: Klebstoff
5 it does not wash off for days: es lässt sich tagelang nicht abwaschen
6 chemical mixture: chemische Mischung
7 to set a trap: eine Falle stellen
8 to smear: schmieren

14. The Secret of Duane Carpenter

TR. 14

The Three Investigators get up early. It's still dark outside when they hear Candace Duskin in the shower.
"We can't go in there!" Bob says.
"Maybe she is trying to wash off the paste!" Peter says.
"We have to wait for her!" Justus looks out of a big window. Jared Fox is standing in the snow, putting his bag onto his sled. "Fox wants to leave[1]!" he tells the others.
"But the vet has not checked his dogs yet! They'll disqualify him!" Bob says.
"He's trying to escape[2] with the gold!" Justus opens the door. "Hurry up, Peter. I think we can catch him! You stay here and watch Miss Duskin, Bob!"
Justus and Peter run out of the gym.
When they jump on their ski-doo, it starts to snow. Peter steps on the gas. "I can't see Fox!" he shouts.
"Just follow his tracks[3]!" Justus answers. "And hurry up! The snow will cover[4] them soon!"
After two miles the tracks lead the boys on their ski-doo into the hills. Thousands of snowflakes dance around them. Peter has to concentrate very hard. He can hardly[5] see the tracks on the ground. "I hate winter!" he grumbles.[6]

1 to leave: abfahren
2 to escape: entkommen
3 tracks: Spuren
4 to cover: bedecken, verdecken
5 hardly: kaum
6 to grumble – *hier:* vor sich hin schimpfen

"Where are your friends?" The man who calls himself "Duane Carpenter" walks towards Bob. The Third Investigator is still standing in front of the changing room and the showers.

"They are out for a walk!" Bob answers.

"I don't believe you!" Duane Carpenter says with a stern[1] voice. "Something is going on!"

"No, they really just went for a walk!" Again Bob looks at the door of the changing room. Candace Duskin is still in there.

"Don't lie to me, boy!" Duane Carpenter is angry. "I think you know what is hidden in Baxter Norsworthy's blue box!"

"Yes, we do!" Bob smiles. "But if you think that it's the stolen gold, you're mistaken!"

"It isn't the gold?" Now, Duane Carpenter is surprised. "It must be the gold and Jack London's bag. I'm sure Baxter Norsworthy is the thief!"

"Baxter Norsworthy is not the thief, Sir!" Bob says. Then he adds, "And you aren't a photographer!"

"Well, no, I'm not. But that's not important now! I can't let the thief get away with the gold!" says Duane Carpenter. "Who stole it? Candace Duskin? Gordon Hoke? Or Francis Studstill? Do you know?" He looks at Bob.

"Well, I won't tell you anything until you tell me who you are!" Bob answers.

"All right, I'll tell you!" Duane Carpenter sighs. "You are right: Duane Carpenter is not my real name. My name is George Bennett and I work as a detective for an insurance company[2]." He shows Bob his ID card,[3] then he adds: "The museum in Dawson hired[4] me."

"And we thought you were[5] a criminal!" Bob says. He smiles.

1 stern: streng
2 insurance company: Versicherungsfirma
3 ID card: Ausweis
4 to hire: einstellen
5 we thought you were: wir dachten, Sie wären

"I thought **you** boys were[1] criminals," Duane Carpenter alias George Bennett answers.
"Of course not! We are private investigators!" Bob tells him.
"And what did you find out?" the detective asks.
"Jared Fox has the gold. That is why he hit Candace Duskin in Beaver Falls. And today he left Stone before the vet checked his dogs!"
"He left?" The detective doesn't like that information.
"But Justus and Peter followed him!" Bob says.
"That's dangerous!" shouts George Bennett. He seems to be concerned[2]. "Fox might have a weapon! And there is a blizzard coming! It isn't safe to be out in the wilderness alone! We have to help them!" The detective opens the door. "Come with me!"
"But I can't, Sir. I have a job to do!" Bob says.
"I think it's more important that you save[3] your friends, Bob!"
"You're right, Mr Carpenter ... I mean ... Mr Bennett! But first, I have to go and talk to Carol and the other mushers! They need to know the truth about Candace Duskin. She's the saboteur!"
"Okay, Bob. I'll meet you outside in five minutes! And ask Carol to join us! The more people we are, the better[4]!"

Detective Question 14

Why did George Bennett pretend to be a photographer called Duane Carpenter?

1 I thought you boys were: ich dachte, ihr Jungen wärt
2 he seems to be concerned: er scheint besorgt zu sein
3 to save: retten
4 the more ... the better: je mehr ... desto besser

15. The Ghost Town

TR. 15

"Where is he going?" Peter asks. He stops his ski-doo at the top of a hill.

"There is a ghost town down there!" Justus points at the foot of a rocky[1] hill. "It must be an old gold mine. I think Jared Fox is going to meet somebody."

"To give him the gold and Jack London's bag?" Peter looks at his friend.

"Yes! And I think I know who Jared Fox is going to meet. But there's no time to explain. Let 's go!"

They drive down the hill. Behind a group of trees, they find Fox's sled and his dogs. One of them barks.

"Hush!" Peter whispers.

"Fox must be close[2]!" Justus points at several[3] footprints in the snow. They lead to a couple of old wooden houses. The buildings have broken windows and some of them also have broken roofs[4]. One of the houses is much bigger than the others. It's four stories[5] high and its back side is built[6] right into the hill. Several feet[7] above the ground there is a long balcony[8].

"Fox is inside that house," Justus whispers. "We have to be careful! He must not see us!" Carefully he sneaks towards the building. Peter follows him. "I hear people talking! I think there are three or four men in the house."

1 rocky: felsig
2 to be close: in der Nähe sein
3 several: mehrere
4 roof: Dach
5 storey: Stockwerk
6 is built: ist gebaut
7 foot: Fuß (Längenmaß), 1 Fuß = 30,48 cm
8 balcony: Balkon

"We have to get closer!" Justus climbs the hill behind the house. "If we step onto the balcony, we can listen to Fox and the others!"
"But this is too dangerous!" Peter whispers.
"This is the only way we can hear what they are talking about!" Justus pants[1]. It wasn't easy to climb the rocky hill.
"Be careful, Justus! The balcony looks unsound[2]!" Peter says. "Maybe you're too heavy for the balcony. I don't want you to break through its floor!" "I'm not **that** fat!" Justus answers angrily. "I'm just a little bit stocky! That's all." He steps onto the balcony. Through one of the broken windows he hears a male[3] voice.
"I can't understand what he's saying!" Justus whispers.
"Me neither[4]!" Peter sneaks across the balcony towards the next window. The floor creaks[5] beneath his feet.
"Don't go there!" Justus warns his friend.
"I can do this!" Peter whispers. "You know that I'm very athletic. And to be honest: I'm less heavy than you are!" Just when he says those words, the floor breaks underneath[6] his feet. Peter is so surprised, he doesn't grab[7] a piece of wood to hold on to[8]. Before he even knows what's happening, he falls down!

Detective Question 15

Why does Peter climb onto the balcony?

1 to pant: schnaufen
2 unsound – hier: morsch
3 male: männlich
4 me neither: ich auch nicht
5 to creak: knarren
6 underneath: unter
7 to grab something: etwas packen
8 to hold on to something: (sich) an etwas festhalten

16. Caught!

TR. 16

Peter hits the ground. For a short moment, he can't breathe. His arms and legs hurt very much. Peter feels his heart beat[1].

Carefully, he moves his legs. First the right leg, then the left leg. They are okay. Then he moves his right arm. He gasps. That hurts! Peter thinks that it's broken! But he has no time to examine[2] the arm. Four people walk towards him. One of them is Jared Fox, the pale musher! Two young men with guns follow Jared Fox. And then there is another man: Jonathan Woodland, the boss of "Kodiak Sports" – the man with the gold nugget and the private gold rush museum.

"It seems we have guests!" Mr Woodland looks at Peter and Justus. Then he turns around to one of the men. "Wellford, make sure[3] there are no other people around[4]!"

"Yes, Sir!" Mr Wellford says and walks away.

"The weather is terrible," Mr Woodland smiles. "I think we should go inside!" He looks at Justus. "Please, come down, boy!"

Justus climbs off[5] the balcony. He is angry. This is a bad situation!

Mr Wellford, the young man with the gun, comes back to the group. He says, "There are no other people, Sir!"

"So, let's go inside!" Mr Woodland slowly walks into the house. Justus and Peter follow him.

"I knew it was you who stole the gold and the bag!" Justus says to Mr Woodland.

"Did you? Ah, then tell me how you found out," Mr Woodland sits down.

1 to beat: schlagen
2 to examine: untersuchen
3 to make sure: sich versichern
4 around – *hier*: in der Nähe
5 to climb off: heruntersteigen

"Well, first you are a collector of gold rush artifacts. So, I guess you really wanted Jack London's bag!"
"Yes, Jack London is my favourite writer! But is that all?" Mr Woodland asks Justus.
"No, there are other clues that lead to you[1]!" Justus explains. "A normal thief would hide[2] the gold and the bag in Dawson until spring. Then he would drive away. But you are an adventurer! You didn't want to wait. You asked a musher to take the stolen things and to bring them here – to an old ghost town with a gold mine! It's just a game for you!"
"You are absolutely right!" Mr Woodland smiles. "You are a clever boy! Unfortunately I can't stay and talk to you. I heard that a blizzard is coming. So I have to fly back to Anchorage!"
"And… what will happen to us?" Peter asks.
"I will let you go!" Mr Woodland gets up.
"Really?" Peter doesn't believe[3] him.
"Yes! But you have to go without your ski-doos. You walk through the blizzard. If you are lucky you'll arrive at that little town Stone tomorrow."
"We could freeze to death[4]!" Justus says.
"I know! What a shame[5]! But maybe you will be rescued[6]."
"You can't let them go!" Jared Fox shouts. "They will tell the police!"
"Nobody will believe them. Besides, they can't prove that we stole the gold and the bag."
"Still, I wouldn't let them go!" Jared Fox grabs a gun.

1 to lead to someone/something: zu jemandem/etwas führen
2 to hide: verstecken
3 to believe someone: jemandem glauben
4 to freeze to death: erfrieren
5 what a shame: wie schade
6 to be rescued: gerettet werden

"You can't shoot them, Fox. That would be murder!" Mr Woodland says.
"I don't know what to do!" Jared Fox says.
"Well, then just stay here and think about it. I have to go!" Mr Woodland slowly walks towards the door. "Goodbye Mr Fox, and goodbye boys!"

Bob, the detective and Carol drive through the forest. It isn't snowing anymore. "I can see their tracks!" Bob says.
"They lead to a ghost town!" the detective points north. "I know that place. It's called Broken Knee Creek."
"Duane ... I mean ... George, do you think that Fox took the gold to Broken Knee Creek?" Carol asks.
"I'm sure!" the detective answers. "We should drive around the hill and walk to the town from the other side. I know the area[1]. There are places where we can hide."
"But what are we going to do then, Mr. Bennett?" Bob asks.
"We hide until they go back to their plane or their sleds." He shows them a pistol. "As you see, I have a weapon."

Behind the ghost town Broken Knee Creek they find a small plane. It's standing on a frozen lake[2]. George Bennett, the detective, climbs into the cockpit.
"There is a radio in the plane! I'm going to call the police!"
"But we have to help Peter and Justus!" Bob says.
"We will, Bob," George Bennett turns on the radio and contacts[3] the police. He tells them where they are and asks for help[4]. They promise to come as soon as possible. After that, the detective searches the plane for weapons. He finds an old gun.

1 area: Gegend
2 lake: See
3 to contact: kontaktieren
4 to ask for help: um Hilfe bitten

"You take that!" He hands Bob the weapon.
"I hate guns and besides, I don't even know how to fire one!" says Bob.
"Then don't shoot! Just hold it! Maybe that's enough to scare[1] the criminals!" George Bennett walks towards a big rock. "Now we have to wait until they all come out!"

Jared Fox is sweating[2]. He is nervous.
"Please, lay the gun down[3], Mr Fox!" Justus says.
The musher shakes his head.
"You are no murderer!" Justus tells him. "You are a musher!"
"But I lose all the time! I can't win the race! And now you are going to tell the police that I helped a criminal[4]! They will arrest me and I will end up in prison!"
"Mr Fox, you did something wrong, that's true. But don't make it worse!" Justus looks at the gun in Fox's hands. He tells himself to stay calm. He takes a deep breath[5]. Justus knows that panic will not help them.
"Mr Fox!" he says again. "Don't make a mistake! Please!"
But Mr Fox lifts the gun and points[6] it at Justus.

Detective Question 16

Why does Mr Woodland let the boys go?

1 to scare someone: jemandem Angst machen
2 to sweat: schwitzen
3 to lay the gun down: das Gewehr niederlegen
4 criminal: Verbrecher
5 to take a deep breath: tief durchatmen
6 to point the gun at someone: das Gewehr auf jemanden richten

17. Bob, the Monster

TR. 17

"They are coming!" George Bennett whispers. He lifts his pistol. Three men walk down the hill. Bob is surprised to see Mr Woodland.
"Now!" George Bennett, the detective, says. He jumps into the open[1]. "Freeze[2]!"
The men stop. Bob points his gun at them. He feels terrible. He knows that he can't shoot, even if something happens.
"Lay your guns down! Then put your hands up!" the detective shouts. The men do what he tells them. Mr Woodland and the others put their guns on the ground. Then they lift their arms.
"Now, Carol, collect their weapons!" George Bennett says to the reporter.
Carol Ford nods and walks towards Woodland and his two men. She takes the guns, then she fetches a rope from the plane. "I'll tie up[3] the criminals with this rope!" she tells Bob and Mr Bennett.
"Where are Justus and Peter?" Bob asks Mr Woodland.
"Well," Mr Woodland answers, "they are having a little talk with a nice musher!" He laughs.
"I am warning you, Woodland!" George Bennett says with an angry voice. "Tell us the truth!"
"They are in the big red house!" Woodland points up the hill. "It's the house next to the old mine!"
"I'll go and help them!" Bob says.
"Let's wait for the police!" George Bennett says to Bob. "I can't leave now! I have to keep an eye on the criminals!"
"Then I'll go without you!" Bob takes his gun and walks up the hill. When he arrives at the top, it starts to snow again. Beneath him, Bob

1 the open – *hier*: das Freie
2 Freeze!: Keine Bewegung! (feste Redewendung)
3 to tie someone up: jemanden fesseln

sees the houses of Broken Knee Creek. The big red house stands a hundred yards away from him. Bob sneaks through the snow. After eighty yards, he hides behind a bush. Bob is happy that there are no windows at this side of the house, so nobody can see him coming. He creeps forward. Luck is on his side! When he arrives at the house he finds a little hole in the wooden wall. He peers[1] through it. Inside the house he can see his friends Justus and Peter. Peter is holding his arm in a strange position. Bob thinks that the arm is hurt, maybe broken! Then he sees Jared Fox and his gun! Bob can't wait. He has to do something! Then, the Third Investigator has an idea. He whistles[2] like a small bird. This is The Three Investigators' special signal. When Justus and Peter hear him whistle, they know that he is there!

They hear a bird whistle. "What's that?" Jared Fox is surprised.
"A bird!" Peter says.
"In the middle of the winter? I don't believe that!" Fox answers.
"It could be a monster!" Justus says with a very loud voice. He hopes that Bob hears him. "Maybe it's the witches! Or maybe a goblin, or a monster! Who knows!"
They hear a spooky sound. Outside, something wails[3] and growls. Justus tries not to laugh. Bob is doing a good job!
"It's a monster!" Justus says to Jared Fox.
"I have to get away!" Now, Jared Fox is frightened. "They have found me! The monsters are coming for me[4]!" He turns around. Peter jumps forward. He grabs Fox's gun. "Ouch!" He nearly drops[5] the gun. "My arm!"
"I'll help you!" Justus takes the gun. "Okay! I have it!" He turns to the musher. "Hands up, Mr Fox!"

1 to peer: spähen
2 to whistle: pfeifen
3 to wail: heulen
4 to come for someone – *hier*: jemanden holen kommen
5 to drop: fallenlassen

Bob enters the room[1]. "I'm here with Carol and an insurance detective! We caught Mr Woodland and called the police! They will arrive soon!"
"Thank you for your help!" Justus says.
"I'm glad you aren't hurt!" Bob smiles.
"Well, actually I am hurt!" Peter touches his right arm carefully. "I need to see a doctor!"

Detective Question 17

How does Bob get the idea to pretend to be a monster?

1 to enter the room: den Raum betreten

18. A Prison full of People

TR. 18

It's already dark when they all arrive at Little Jackson, the next town. Nobody is out on the streets. A strong wind is blowing and big snowflakes are falling. The blizzard is coming.

An old sheriff with a gray beard takes them to the small police station. There, he locks[1] Mr Woodland and his accomplices[2] into two cells. "In all my years as a sheriff I've never had so many people in here!" he says. They sit down in his office. The sheriff offers them coffee and cookies. Suddenly, Justus jumps up. "I hope there's room for one more person!" he says. "We nearly forgot our other case!"

"Yes!" Bob says. "The sabotage! Sir, do you know where the mushers are right now?"

"They are not allowed to continue[3] driving, because of the blizzard. They have to stay in the fire station[4]. There is enough room for everybody and the townspeople[5] organized a party for them."

"Then we have to go to the fire station!" Justus says to Bob.

"But we have to wait for Peter!" Bob says. The Second Investigator is not with them. He has gone to the local doctor.

Justus and Bob go to the doctor's house. But Peter isn't there anymore.

"Your friend went to the fire station." the doctor tells them. "You just missed[6] him!"

1 to lock someone into a cell: jemanden in einer Zelle einschließen
2 accomplice: Verbündeter
3 they are not allowed to do something: es ist ihnen nicht erlaubt, etwas zu tun
4 fire station: Feuerwache
5 townspeople: die Bewohner der Stadt
6 to miss someone – *hier:* jemanden verpassen

There is a lot of snow on the streets and the wind is strong. Bob is happy that the doctor lives next to the fire station. This way[1], they don't have to walk far.

Inside the building local women offer soup and hot drinks to the mushers. A band is playing.

"Nice party!" Bob says.

"There he is!" Justus points at Peter. He has a cast[2] on his arm but he seems quite happy.

"I just solved[3] our second case!" he says. Peter is proud.

"What?" Justus is surprised.

"Yes, I went over to Candace Duskin. I looked at her. And guess what I saw! There are black stains on her fingers!"

"Our plan worked[4]!" Justus smiles.

"I said to her: "Miss Duskin, I know that you are the saboteur!" At first she denied[5] it but now she understands that the stains on her hands are evidence[6] enough!"

"How did she react?" Bob asks.

"She started to cry!" Peter looks at a bench where Gordon Hoke and Baxter Norsworthy are sitting together with Candace Duskin. "They are keeping an eye on her[7] until the police arrive. I've called the sheriff!"

Justus walks over to Miss Duskin. She is trying to rub the stains off her hands.

"It won't work!" Justus tells her. "The stains will stay there for several days!"

1 this way – *hier:* so
2 cast: Gips
3 to solve: lösen
4 to work – *hier:* funktionieren
5 to deny something: etwas abstreiten
6 evidence: Beweismaterial
7 to keep an eye on someone: ein Auge auf jemanden haben, jemanden beobachten

The blond woman looks at him with anger in her eyes. "What is it? I can't get it off my fingers[1]! It's terrible!"
"Well, the paste is one of my special inventions[2]!" Justus says proudly. Then he gives her The Three Investigators' card.

The Three Investigators
We take on any case
First Investigator Justus Jonas
Second Investigator Peter Shaw
Research and Archives Bob Andrews

"I don't want your stupid card!" Miss Duskin growls.
"Take it, Candace!" Baxter Norsworthy smiles. "Then you'll have something to read when you are in prison!"

Detective Question 18

How did Candace Duskin get the paste on her hands? (Tip: You have to remember what happened in the earlier chapters to answer this question.)

1 to get something off something: etwas von etwas abbekommen
2 invention: Erfindung

19. An arctic Memory

TR. 19

One day later, Baxter Norsworthy and his dogs arrive at the finish line[1] in Fairbanks. But he doesn't win the race. Because of the sabotage the organizers of the "Nordic Wilderness Race" decide that the race has to be repeated[2] next winter.

Carol still films some of the mushers who drive into Fairbanks. Meanwhile Bob goes to a shop to get a present for Jelena. He buys her a little pencil case that looks like a bear. Justus tells him: "I will keep it safe until we get back to Rocky Beach!" Then, when Bob leaves the room, he puts it in the bag with their dirty clothes.

The next evening they all meet at a restaurant. Carol treats them[3] to a meal.

"You really deserve a reward[4]!" George Bennett – the detective who called himself Duane Carpenter- tells The Three Investigators.

"We got one!" Justus tells him. "The museum and the collectors are very grateful[5] that we solved the case. So they plan to give us a nice sum of money[6]."

"We are going to save it for college[7]!" Peter says.

"But actually, I think we will have to spend it on our office in Rocky Beach. We have to pay for our telephone, the internet and the electricity."

1 finish line: Ziellinie, Zielgerade
2 to be repeated: wiederholt werden
3 to treat someone to something: jemanden einladen, jemandem einen ausgeben
4 reward: Belohnung
5 grateful: dankbar
6 a nice sum of money: eine ordentliche Menge Geld
7 college: Universität

Baxter Norsworthy laughs. "You should use candles and smoke signals[1]. That is a lot cheaper than electric lights and telephone and internet!"
They all laugh.
"Anyway," Carol says after a short while, "it was great that you came and helped us! Thank you so much!"
"You're welcome[2]!" Justus smiles.
"By the way," Peter reaches[3] into his bag. "I have something for you, Justus."
"Really? What is it?"
"It's a gift! A souvenir[4] of our case in Alaska!" With his left hand Peter holds up a bottle of "Arctic Autumn".
"Oh please, not that terrible stuff!" Justus doesn't look happy. But before he can do anything, Peter sprays the antiperspirant at his friend.
"The smell of the wilderness – for just three dollars and ninety cents!" Peter says.
Justus coughs, but then he can't help it[5] – he has to laugh – and all the others laugh too.

Detective Question 19

Which of The Three Investigators is your favourite detective and why?

1 smoke signals: Rauchsignale
2 you are welcome: gern geschehen
3 to reach – hier: greifen
4 souvenir: Andenken
5 he can't help it: er kann es nicht verhindern

Englisch-Deutsche Wortliste

accident – *Unfall*
accomplice – *Verbündeter, Mittäter*
ache – *schmerzen*
add – *hinzufügen*
adventurer – *Abenteurer*
alarmed (to be) – *erschrocken (sein)*
all of a sudden – *auf einmal*
allowed (to do something) – *erlaubt (etwas zu tun)*
ancient culture – *antike Kultur*
antiperspirant – *Deodorant*
appear – *erscheinen*
area – *Gegend*
argue – *argumentieren, streiten*
around – *1. um, herum 2. in der Nähe*
arrested (to be) – *festgenommen (werden)*
ask for help – *um Hilfe bitten*
at a speed of – *mit einer Geschwindigkeit von*
attack – *angreifen*
balcony – *Balkon*
band-aid – *Pflaster*
bark – *bellen*
be close – *in der Nähe sein*
be into something – *sich für etwas begeistern*
beat – *schlagen, besiegen*
beauty contest – *Schönheitswettbewerb*
behave like – *sich verhalten wie*
believe someone – *jemandem glauben*
bench – *Bank*

besides – *außerdem*
bet – *wetten*
blanket – *Decke*
bloodstained – *blutbefleckt*
blur pictures – *unscharfe Fotos machen*
blurred – *verschwommen, unscharf*
boil – *(Wasser) kochen*
bucket – *Eimer*
burn (one's eyes) – *(in den Augen) brennen*
busy – *beschäftigt*
by means of – *mittels*
cabin – *(Holz)hütte, Holzhaus*
calm somebody down – *jemanden beruhigen*
camp – *Lager*
caribou – *Karibu (nordamerikanisches Rentier)*
case – *Fall*
cast – *Gips*
catch – *1. fangen 2. bekommen, angesteckt werden*
changing room – *Umkleideraum*
chemical mixture – *chemische Mischung*
chest – *Brustkorb*
climb off – *heruntersteigen*
clue – *Anhaltspunkt*
collide – *zusammenprallen*
come for someone – *jemanden holen kommen, wegen jemandem kommen*
complain – *sich beschweren*
concerned – *besorgt*
contact – *kontaktieren*
cope with – *zurechtkommen mit*
cough – *husten*

cover – *bedecken, verdecken*
crack – *Sprung, Riss*
crackle – *knistern, knacken*
crackle – *das Knistern, Knacken*
creak – *knarren*
criminal – *Verbrecher, Krimineller*
crowded – *gedrängt, voll, überfüllt*
curious – *neugierig*
curse – *fluchen*
dare to disturb someone – *es wagen, jemanden zu stören*
decide – *beschließen*
degree – *Grad*
demand – *verlangen*
deny – *abstreiten, bestreiten*
departure – *Abfahrt, Abreise*
desperate – *verzweifelt*
destroy – *zerstören*
dial – *wählen*
directory enquiries – *Telefonauskunft*
disappointed – *enttäuscht*
disqualified – *disqualifiziert*
dizzy – *schwindelig*
do without something – *ohne etwas auskommen*
drip – *tropfen*
drop something – *etwas fallenlassen*
drop – *Tropfen*
drown – *ertrinken*
edge – *Rand*
embarassed (to be) – *verlegen (sein)*
enemy – *Feind, Gegner*
enter – *betreten, eintreten*

entry – *Eintrag*
equipment – *Ausstattung, Werkzeug*
escape – *entkommen*
event – *Veranstaltung, Ereignis*
evidence – *Beweismaterial*
examine – *untersuchen*
exhibition – *Ausstellung*
fairy tale – *Märchen*
feel uncomfortable – *sich unwohl fühlen*
fetch – *holen*
fierce – *wild*
finally – *endlich*
finish line – *Zielgerade*
fire station – *Feuerwache*
flare gun – *Leuchtpistole*
flashlight – *Taschenlampe*
food poisoning – *Lebensmittelvergiftung*
foot – *Fuß, (Längenmaß) 1 Fuß = 30,48 cm*
footprints – *Fußspuren*
for days – *tagelang*
forehead – *Stirn*
freckles – *Sommersprossen*
freeze to death – *erfrieren*
Freeze! – *Keine Bewegung!*
frozen to death – *erfroren*
fuel – *Benzin, Treibstoff*
gas station – *Tankstelle*
gasp – *nach Luft schnappen*
gather – *sammeln*
gathered (to be) – *versammelt (sein)*
get something off something – *etwas von etwas abbekommen*

glance – *Blick*
gleam – *leuchten*
glowing – *leuchtend*
glue – *Klebstoff*
goblin – *Kobold, Gnom*
gold digger – *Goldgräber*
goosebumps – *Gänsehaut*
grab something – *etwas packen*
grateful – *dankbar*
growl – *knurren*
grumble – *murren, vor sich hinschimpfen*
guess – *raten, schätzen, vermuten*
gun – *Gewehr*
gym – *Turnhalle*
hardly – *kaum*
harm someone – *jemandem schaden*
have a hard time – *es schwer haben, Probleme haben*
have a mind of one's own – *seinen eigenen Kopf haben*
hide – *(sich) verstecken*
hire – *einstellen*
hit the brakes – *auf die Bremse treten, bremsen*
hold on to something – *sich an etwas festhalten*
hood – *Kapuze*
howl – *heulen*
huge – *riesig*
hurry – *sich beeilen*
hush – *psst, ruhig*
ID card – *Ausweis*
in a rush (to be) – *in Eile (sein)*
in his late fifites – *Ende fünfzig*
inhabitant – *Einwohner, Bewohner*

inspect – *untersuchen*
instead – *statt dessen*
insurance company – *Versicherungsgesellschaft*
internet access – *Internetzugang*
interrupt – *unterbrechen*
introduce someone – *jemanden vorstellen*
invention – *Erfindung*
investigate – *untersuchen, ermitteln*
investigator – *Ermittler*
involved (to be) – *beteiligt (sein)*
item – *Stück*
jackrabbit – *Hase*
keep an eye on someome – *ein Auge auf jemanden haben*
kneel down – *niederknien, sich hinknien*
lack of – *Mangel an*
lake – *See*
launch – *starten*
lead to someone/something – *zu jemandem/etwas führen*
leave – *abfahren, abreisen, weggehen*
lecture – *Vorlesung, Vortrag*
lie to someone – *jemanden anlügen*
lift – *heben*
light a fire – *ein Feuer anzünden*
local – *örtlich*
loss – *Verlust*
luggage – *Gepäck*
magical impact – *magische Wirkung*
make sure – *sich versichern*
male – *männlich*
manage to sleep – *es schaffen, zu schlafen*
marked trail – *markierter Pfad, markierte Strecke*

mat – *Matte*
match – *Streichholz*
me neither – *ich auch nicht*
mess with someone – *sich mit jemanden anlegen*
miss someone – *1. jemanden vermissen 2. jemanden verpassen*
moose – *Elch*
moreover – *außerdem*
most definitely – *ganz bestimmt*
mountain top – *Berggipfel*
mug – *Becher, Tasse*
mumble – *nuscheln, murmeln*
mustn't know – *darf nicht erfahren*
nasty – *gemein, eklig*
nevertheless – *trotzdem*
nice sum of money – *ordentliche Menge Geld*
nod – *nicken*
nugget – *Goldklumpen*
obviously – *offensichlich*
opponent – *Gegner*
otherwise – *ansonsten*
out of breath – *außer Atem*
out of control – *außer Kontrolle*
owl – *Eule*
own – *besitzen*
pale – *blass*
pant – *schnaufen, hecheln*
paste – *Paste*
pat – *tätscheln*
paw – *Pfote*
peer – *spähen*
phone booth – *Telefonzelle*

place – *platzieren*
point the gun at someone – *das Gewehr auf jemanden richten*
pool – *Lache*
possible – *möglich*
prepare dinner – *das Abendessen zubereiten*
prepared – *vorbereitet*
press office – *Pressestelle*
pretend – *so tun als ob*
promise – *versprechen*
properly – *vernünftig, richtig*
prospector – *Goldsucher*
prove – *beweisen*
psychic – *Medium*
psychic (to be) – *übersinnliche Fähigkeiten haben*
purple – *violett*
qualify – *sich qualifizieren (für einen Wettkampf oder einen Job)*
quit – *aufhören*
ranger – *Förster*
raw – *roh*
reach for something – *nach etwas greifen*
reach – *erreichen*
react – *reagieren*
recognize – *erkennen*
reflect – *reflektieren, wiederspiegeln*
reins – *Zügel*
rely on – *sich verlassen auf*
repeated (to be) – *wiederholt (werden)*
rescued (to be) – *gerettet (werden)*
restroom – *Toilette*
retire – *in Ruhestand gehen*
return – *zurückkommen*

reward someone – *jemanden belohnen*
reward – *Belohnung*
rocky – *felsig*
roof – *Decke*
rough – *rau, heiser*
rub – *reiben*
ruin – *ruinieren, verderben*
rumour – *Gerücht*
saboteur – *Saboteur*
save – *retten*
scare someone – *jemandem Angst machen*
scarf – *Schal*
screen – *überprüfen*
search for – *suchen (nach)*
seem – *scheinen*
self-confidence – *Selbstbewusstsein*
serious – *ernst*
set on fire – *anzünden*
set a trap – *eine Falle stellen*
several – *mehrere*
severe – *1.streng 2.stark, heftig*
shiver – *zittern, schaudern*
show off – *angeben*
shudder – *schaudern, zittern*
shut up – *still sein, das Maul halten (umgangssprachlich)*
sigh – *seufzen*
sign – *Zeichen*
sink – *Waschbecken*
sip – *Schluck*
ski-doo – *Schneemobil*
slam – *knallen*

sled-dog race – *Schlittenhundrennen*
slide – *rutschen*
smear – *schmieren*
smoke signal – *Rauchsignal*
smoke – *Rauch*
sneak – *schleichen*
sniff – *riechen, schnüffeln*
snowflake – *Schneeflocke*
solve – *lösen*
sore – *wund, schmerzhaft*
souvenir – *Andenken*
sparkle – *glitzern*
special – *besonders*
spill – *verschütten*
splash – *spritzen*
spooky – *gruselig*
spot – *bemerken*
stain – *Fleck*
step on the gas – *auf das Gaspedal treten, Gas geben*
stern – *streng, ernst*
stocky – *stämmig*
stomach ache – *Bauchschmerzen*
storey – *Stockwerk*
stove – *Ofen*
stuffed toy – *Stofftier*
suggest – *vorschlagen*
suspect – *Verdächtige(r)*
suspect – *verdächtigen*
suspicious – *verdächtig*
swear – *fluchen*
sweat – *schwitzen*

take a break – *eine Pause machen*
take a deep breath – *tief durchatmen*
take down notes – *Notizen machen*
take part in – *teilnehmen an*
talisman – *Talisman, Glücksbringer*
tame – *zahm*
this way – *auf diese Art und Weise, so*
tie someone up – *jemanden fesseln*
tip over – *umkippen*
torch – *Fackel*
towards – *auf etwas zu*
townspeople – *Bewohner der Stadt*
tracks – *Spuren*
trail – *1. Spur 2. Pfad, (Wander)weg*
trail sign – *Wegweiser*
treasure – *Schatz*
treat someone to something – *jemanden einladen, jemandem einen ausgeben*
tripod – *Stativ*
twig – *Zweig*
tuck one's tail between one's legs – *den Schwanz einziehen*
unconscious – *bewusstlos*
underestimate – *unterschätzen*
underneath – *unter*
unsound – *morsch*
valuable – *wertvoll*
vanish – *verschwinden*
veterinarian (kurz: vet) – *Tierarzt/Tierärtzin*
victim – *Opfer*
view – *Aussicht*
wail – *heulen*

walk over to someone – *zu jemandem herübergehen*
wave – *winken*
weapon – *Waffe*
what a shame – *wie schade*
what something is like – *wie etwas ist*
whine – *winseln*
whisper – *flüstern*
whistle – *pfeifen*
whole – *ganz*
witch – *Hexe*
wonder – *sich fragen*
work – *1. arbeiten 2. funktionieren*
wound – *Wunde*
wrap up – *einwickeln*
yard – *Hof*
yard – *angloamerikanische Längeneinheit – 91,44 cm*
yawn – *gähnen*
yeti – *Yeti*
you are welcome – *gern geschehen*
you wish – *das hättest du wohl gerne (umgangssprachlich)*

Nützliche Detektiv-Ausdrücke

Hier sind einige Vokabeln und Redewendungen, die hilfreich sind, wenn man über Verbrechen und Detektivarbeit spricht

arrest someone – *jemanden festnehmen*
be sent to prison – *ins Gefängnis gesteckt werden*
break into a house/museum – *in ein Haus/Museum einbrechen*
case – *Fall*
collect evidence – *Beweismaterial/Hinweise sammeln*
commit a crime – *ein Verbrechen begehen*
commit sabotage – *Sabotage begehen*
criminal – *Krimineller, Verbrecher*
detective – *Detektiv*
discover a clue – *einen Hinweis entdecken*
drop one's weapon – *seine Waffe fallen lassen*
evidence – *Beweismaterial*
Freeze! – *Keine Bewegung!*
guilty – *schuldig*
innocent – *unschuldig*
investigate a case – *in einem Fall ermitteln*
investigation – *Ermittlung*
investigator – *ein Ermittler, eine Ermittlerin*
launch an investigation – *eine Ermittlung starten*
look out for something – *auf etwas achten*
point a gun/pistol at someone – *ein Gewehr/eine Pistole auf jemanden richten*
prove that someone is guilty/innocent – *beweisen, dass jemand schuldig/unschuldig ist*
robbery – *ein Raubüberfall, ein Diebstahl*

solve a case – *einen Fall lösen*
steal something – *etwas stehlen*
suspect – *ein Verdächtiger, eine Verdächtige*
suspicious behaviour – *verdächtiges Verhalten*
suspicious person – *eine verdächtige Person*
thief – *Dieb*
tie someone up – *jemanden fesseln*
weapon – *Waffe*

Übungen

Chapter 1:

1. Key words

Schau dir die Wörter und die 3 Erklärungen an. Welche ist die richtige?

1. saboteur
a) someone who steals things
b) someone who does criminal things to stop other people from doing something
c) someone who does not like dogs and tries to hurt them

2. investigator
a) a reporter
b) a camera man
c) a detective

3. musher
a) a person who lives in Alaska
b) a person who owns one or more huskies
c) a person who drives a sled with dogs

2. Who's who?

Verbinde die Beschreibung mit dem richtigen Namen:

1. A small red-haired woman
2. A musher who is rude and thinks he is the best musher in the world
3. A musher who believes in monsters and ghosts
4. A reporter who thinks that there is a saboteur in the race

a) Carol Ford
b) Jared Fox
c) Baxter Norsworthy
d) Francis Studstill

3. Fill in the blanks

Ergänze die Sätze mit den fehlenden Wörtern:

1. The sled dog race starts in ________ and finishes in ________.
2. Four mushers cannot take part in the race because they or their dogs are ________.
3. Carol's old camera team got ________ ________ after they ate some cookies.
4. The winner of the race will do ________ for "Kodiak Sports" or "Apollo Dog-food".

Chapter 2:

4. Thief!

In diesem kurzen Text fehlen einige wichtige Informationen über den Diebstahl in Dawsons Museum. Kannst du die Lücken mit den richtigen Wörtern füllen?

1. Somebody stole a bucket full of ________ and a ________ from the museum.
2. Carol says the thief could not leave Dawson because there was a ________ on the night he stole the bag.
3. Now, the thief can't leave because the ________ are checking every car that leaves the town.
4. Carol is angry because nobody cares about the ________ anymore, because they are thinking about the stolen gold.

5. Gold!

Verbinde die Erklärung mit dem richtigen Wort:

1. a lump of gold	a) exhibition
2. someone who is looking for gold	b) gold mine
3. worth a lot of money	c) nugget
4. a place where people dig for gold	d) gold digger/prospector
5. a special show in a museum	e) valuable

Chapter 3:

6. What's wrong?

Hier sind einige Informationen aus dem dritten Kapitel. Aber es haben sich ein paar Fehler eingeschlichen. Streiche die falschen Informationen:

Mr Woodland is a sponsor for the race. He is also the man who owns the bag which was stolen from the museum. When he was young, he was a teacher.
Baxter Norsworthy has a black coat and a red sled. He is very friendly and polite.
Candace Duskin is tall and blond. She is the only woman in the race.

7. Word Chain

Finde alle Wörter, die sich im Polarlicht versteckt haben.

olmushergfpsychicsndprospectorbiumartifactums

embarrassedercheerosslossowcrowdedew

Chapter 4:

8. Camping equipment

Versuche, eine Liste mit mindestens fünf Dingen zu erstellen, die man beim Camping braucht (natürlich auf Englisch!).

____

____

____

____

____

9. Animal world

Hier ist eine Liste mit Tieren. Welche davon sehen oder hören die drei ??? in Kapitel 4?

wolf
fox
moose
jackrabbit
puma
owl
bear

Tipp!
Wenn du nicht sicher bist, wie die Tiere auf deutsch heiβen, kannst du im Wörterbuch oder unter www.pons.eu nachschlagen.

Chapter 5:

10. Ways to say "say"

In diesem Kapitel findest du viele verschiedene Wörter, die man nach der wörtlichen Rede statt ‚say' verwenden kann. Wähle für jeden Satz ein passendes Wort aus der Liste aus und setze es in die Lücke.

tell, shout, answer, ask, explain, greet, say

Tipp!
Denk an die Endung s bei he/she/it.

1. "Bob, be careful!" Carol ________.
2. "It's very cold today," Duane Carpenter ________ to Justus.
3. "Good morning. Did you sleep well?" Francis ________ the boys when they climb out of their tents.
4. Peter ________, "Has anyone seen my sleeping bag?"
5. "Yes, it's on the ski-doo," Bob ________.
6. "Today, we will drive to the Yukon river," Carol ________ the boys.
7. "When electrons collide with atoms of the upper atmosphere of the earth you get Northern lights," Justus ________ to his friends.

Tipp!
Anders als im Deutschen sind die Anführungszeichen sowohl vor als auch nach der wörtlichen Rede hochgestellt (oben).

11. Detective work

Wärst du auch ein guter Detektiv? Welcher der Hundeschlittenfuehrer ist deiner Meinung nach in Kapitel vier und fünf am verdächtigsten? (Versuche, die Informationen, die du später im Buch bekommst bei dieser Frage außer Acht zu lassen.)

1. Francis is suspicious because she does not want to talk about sabotage and makes fun of Justus when he talks about it.
2. Candace Duskin is suspicious because in detective stories, it's always the nice people who do the bad things.
3. Baxter Norsworthy is suspicious because he wants to win very much and does not care if he hurts other people, for example when he drives past them with his sled.

12. Similar but different

Einige Wörter, die du neu kennengelernt hast, sehen sehr ähnlich (oder sogar gleich!) aus und haben auch sehr ähnliche Bedeutungen:

crime: Verbrechen
criminal: Verbrecher

suspect (n.): Verdächtige(r)
to suspect someone: jemanden verdächtigen
suspicious: verdächtig

Versuche nun, die neuen Wörter zu benutzen. Wähle für jede Lücke das richtige Wort aus der Liste.

Tipp!
Bei dem Substantiv *suspect* (Verdächtiger) ist die Betonung auf der ersten Silbe, im Gegensatz dazu ist die Betonung bei dem Verb *to suspect* (verdächtigen) auf der zweiten Silbe.

suspect (Nomen), suspect (Verb), suspicious, crime, criminal

1. If you steal something or murder someone, that's a ________.
2. When you do not know who has committed the crime, everybody who behaves strangely is ________.
3. A ________ is a person who you think possibly committed the crime.
4. If you think someone is a criminal, you ________ him.
5. A ________ is someone who has committed a crime.

13. Rules for Detectives

Hier sind drei allgemeine Regeln, die beim Lösen eines Kriminalfalls beachtet werden sollten. Darunter sind drei Beispiele, die zeigen, wie die drei ??? diese Regeln anwenden. Welches Beispiel passt zu welcher Regel?

1) Try to discover what motives the criminal might have for the crime.
2) Find as much information as possible about the people who are suspects.
3) Look out for any suspicious actions.

a) The Three Investigators ask Jelena to look up Duane Carpenter and the mushers on the internet.
b) The Three Investigators find out that the winner of the race will get lots of money by doing advertising for the sponsors.
c) Peter decides to watch Baxter Norsworthy.

Chapter 6:

14. Disappointed

In Kapitel 6 sind drei Leute aus unterschiedlich ernsten Gründen enttäuscht. Setze die richtigen Namen in die Lücken.

1. ________ is disappointed because there are no showers at the camp.
2. ________ is disappointed because he is ill and cannot continue with the race.
3. ________ is disappointed because her dog Spooky has a stomach ache and cannot run any longer.

15. On the track

Bis du auf der richtigen Spur? Sortiere die Wörter aus, die nichts mit Winter, Wildnis und Schlittenhunderennen zu tun haben.

palm musher honey sled-
dog cabin sunburn nugget sky-
scraper prospector drown freeze to
death moose

Chapter 7:

16. The best word

Suche das Wort aus, das deiner Meinung nach am Besten in die Lücke passt. Oft gibt es mehr als eine richtige Antwort.

1. When Peter sees the trail of blood he feels angry/shocked/scared.
2. Bob worries that there is a wolf/bear/murderer in the woods.
3. After the attack, Candace Duskin looks pale/ill/scared.
4. Duane Carpenter asks many questions and seems to be excited/bored/shocked.

17. Ice-cold

Im eisig kalten Wind sind ein paar Wörter auseinandergebrochen. Kannst du sie wieder zusammensetzen?

footpri · diz · sn · uncons · bloodsta

band · ited · sne · ead · cious · zy · t

inst · ak · sab · aid · ches · spo · exc

nts · owy · oky · oteur · ined

Chapter 8:

18. Scrambled Letters

Die drei ??? rätseln, was wohl in der Kiste von Baxter Norsworthy sein könnte. Hier ist eine Liste mit einigen Möglichkeiten. Leider sind die Buchstaben durcheinander geraten. Kannst du sie wieder in die richtige Reihenfolge bringen?

1. sinopo	Tip: you can make people ill with it
2. amp	Tip: it helps you find things
3. napewo	Tip: you can attack people with it
4. dolg	Tip: it is very valuable
5. thoselc	Tip: you wear them

19. Investigation

Die drei ??? überlegen, wer hinter dem Anschlag auf Candace Duskin steckt. Peter macht sich Notizen zu ihren Vermutungen, aber er macht dabei ein paar Fehler. Was ist richtig und was falsch?

1. Baxter Norsworthy probably poisoned Spooky.	true ☐	false ☐
2. Norsworthy arrived at Beaver Falls first.	true ☐	false ☐
3. Duane Carpenter didn't lie to us about his camera.	true ☐	false ☐
4. Francis Studstill was asleep alone in a cabin when Miss Duskin was attacked.	true ☐	false ☐
5. To do: Let's check just Mr Norsworthys identity.	true ☐	false ☐

Chapter 9:

20. Snow and Cold Vocabulary

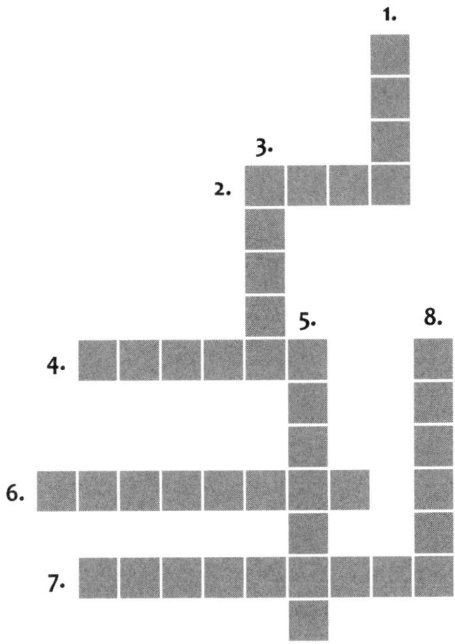

Tipp!
Wenn dir ein Wort nicht einfällt, dann schau doch im Wörterbuch nach oder unter www.pons.de

Across:
2. kalt
4. Spuren
6. Schneesturm
7. Schneeflocke

Down:
1. Schlitten
3. Sprung, Riss
5. glitzern
8. Grad

Chapter 10:

21. Dog Vocab

Schreibe das passende Wort unter die Zeichnung.

1. ____________

2. ____________

3. ____________

4. ____________

5. ____________

growl – howl – bark – tail – paw

Chapter 11:

22. What's the right answer?

Suche die richtige Antwort aus:

1. What do you normally use a flare gun for?
a) To shoot at wolves.
b) To call for help if you are at sea or in a lonely place.
c) To show off in front of your friends.

2. What should you not do with Justus Jonas?
a) Dance with him.
b) Feed him too many cookies.
c) Mess with him.

3. What noise do wolves make?
a) They howl.
b) They wail.
c) They shout.

Chapter 12:

23. Complete the sentence

Jelena übermittelt Bob einige wichtige Informationen, die zu weiteren Vermutungen Anlass geben. In dieser Übung findest du einige Vermutungen samt Erklärung. Leider passen sie nicht immer zusammen. Verbinde die Vermutungen und Erklärungen, die zusammenpassen.

1. It's possible that Duane Carpenter is a criminal
2. Gordon Hoke probably wants to win the race very much
3. Candace Duskin might try to win by sabotage
4. Jared Fox might be trying to win the race by unfair means

a) because the winner gets the advertising contract.
b) because it's his last race.
c) because he is always unlucky and never wins.
d) because he is lying about his job and maybe also about his name.

24. What a terrible mess!

Die Schlittenhunde haben im Schnee gewühlt und dabei versehentlich die Buchstaben etlicher Wörter durcheinandergebracht. Setze sie wieder in die richtige Reihenfolge und schreibe die Übersetzung dazu!

	Wort	Übersetzung
1. acidecnt	____________	____________
2. basotage	____________	____________
3. Maintoun Glirs	____________	____________
4. photogarphre	____________	____________
5. Baevre Sallf	____________	____________
6. ritere	____________	____________

Chapter 13:

25. Bob's not perfect

Bob hat eine Liste mit den Ergebnissen der bisherigen Ermittlung angefertigt. Er hat aber fünf Rechtschreibfehler gemacht, einen in jedem Satz. Kannst du sie finden? Falls du Hilfe brauchst, schau dir die korrigierte Version B) ohne Fehler an und vergleiche sie mit der ursprünglichen Version A) mit Fehlern.

Tipp!
Mit einer Ausnahme sind alle Fehler in Bobs Liste Wörter, die es zwar gibt, die aber nicht diejenigen sind, die er benutzen wollte. Ähnlich geschriebene Wörter zu verwechseln ist ein beliebter Fehler, auf den man achten muss!

A)

1. Candace Duskin is the saboteur, she tried to brake Baxter Norsworthy's sled.
2. Their is a stuffed pig in the blue box.
3. Justus wants to proof that Candace Duskin is the saboteur.
4. Jared Fox hit Candace Duskin because he thought she wanted to steel the gold.
5. The First Investigetor is going to set a trap for Miss Duskin.

B)

1. Candace Duskin is the saboteur, she tried to break Baxter Norsworthy's sled.
2. There is a stuffed pig in the blue box.
3. Justus wants to prove that Candace Duskin is the saboteur.
4. Jared Fox hit Candace Duskin because he thought she wanted to steal the gold.
5. The First Investigator is going to set a trap for Miss Duskin.

Chapter 14:

26. Scrambled sentences

In diesen Sätzen sind die Wörter durcheinander gekommen. Kannst du sie wieder in die richtige Reihenfolge bringen?

1. Jared Fox/want to/Justus and Peter/follow

   ____

   ____

2. to find/the detective George Bennett/the museum/the thief/hired

   ____

   ____

3. what Peter and Justus/says/George Bennett/are doing/is dangerous

   ____

   ____

4. will try/Justus and Peter/Bob, Carol and George Bennett/to help

   ____

   ____

Chapter 15:

27. Find the mistakes

Hier ist eine Beschreibung der Geisterstadt und des alten Hauses, in dem Peter und Justus Jared Fox finden. Aber nicht alle Informationen sind korrekt. Kannst du die Fehler finden?

Many houses in the ghost town have broken windows and roofs. The house where Jared Fox is is much smaller than the other houses. The house is on top of a hill. There is a long balcony several feet above the ground. The balcony is very new and not at all dangerous.

28. Detective's work

Den drei ??? fehlen die Worte! Trage die gesuchten Begriffe in die Lücken ein.

1. A criminal does something forbidden, steals something oder hurts people.

He commits a ______________.

2. Somebody destroys or damages things for his own advantage (Vorteil).

It's ______________.

3. An investigator wants to find the criminal. Before he finds the right person, he gathers information about the crime.

Then he has a ______________.

4. The detective wants to solve the case. He investigates it and searches for the guilty person.

He collects ______________.

5. The investigator has several suspects. But then he discovers that one of them didn't do it.

Then the suspect is ______________.

Chapter 16:

29. Combine

In diesem Kapitel findest du einige zusammengesetzte Ausdrücke und Redewendungen. Kannst du sie richtig kombinieren? Als Hilfe findest du unten die deutschen Übersetzungen.

Tipp! Feste Redewendungen lernt man am besten als Ganzes, vor allem, wenn man aus den Bedeutungen der einzelnen Wörter nicht die Bedeutung der ganzen Redewendung erschließen kann.

1. make	a) for help
2. what	b) a deep breath
3. take	c) a shame
4. point	d) to death
5. lay down	e) the weapon
6. freeze	f) a gun at someone
7. ask	g) sure

sich versichern, wie schade, tief durchatmen, ein Gewehr auf jemanden richten, die Waffe niederlegen, erfrieren, um Hilfe bitten

Chapter 17:

30. Noises

Bob versucht Jared Fox Angst zu machen, indem er gruselige Geräusche macht. Kannst du sie finden? Was für andere Geräusche könnte er noch machen? Versuche, dir so viele wie möglich zu überlegen.

Tipp! Für diese Übung kannst du ein Wörterbuch zur Hilfe nehmen.

___

___

___

___

Chapter 18:

31. Complete the sentences

Welche Wörter passen in die Lücken?

1. Justus ________________ that Candace Duskin was the saboteur.
2. Candace tried to ________________ that she was guilty, but the black ________________ on her hands were evidence against her.
3. The police will ________________ her.
4. She is very ________________ with The Three Investigators and does not want their ________________.
5. The Three Investigators are proud because they solved both ________________.

Chapter 19:

32. Whoops!

In den Sätzen unten haben sich einige Fehler eingeschlichen. Streiche das falsche Wort durch und ersetze es durch ein korrektes.

To find out who the saboteur is, The Three Investigators collect flowers and look out for nice behaviour.
The thief looked into the museum and took a bag of bread.
Jared Fox helped the murderer to get the gold out of Dawson. When Justus and Peter discover that he is a suspect, he points a stick at them.
At the end of the investigation, The Three Investigators find out that Candace Duskin is innocent. They decide that she should be sent to the beach.

When Duane Carpenter sees the criminals, he shouts: 'Move!' and tells them to keep their weapons.

33. Detective Vocab

Hier sind einige Wörter, die man braucht, um über Kriminalfälle und Detektivarbeit zu sprechen. Leider sind die Buchstaben durcheinander geraten. Kannst du sie wieder in die richtige Reihenfolge bringen?

1. vitsoagtirne
2. esca
3. raster
4. lacaminri
5. ehfit
6. idevenec
7. tedivecet

Tipp!
Alle Wörter in dieser Übung findest du auch in der Liste mit dem Vokabular zum Thema Detektive und Verbrecher auf Seite 90.

34. Tidy up!

Der Schneesturm hat einige Sätze der Geschichte durcheinandergewirbelt. Räum auf!

1. in her eyes with anger at him the blond woman looks.
2. it's already the next town when they dark arrive all, at Little Jackson.
3. there isn't anymore Peter.
4. an eye on her they arrive the police until are keeping.
5. a lot of strong snow on the streets there is and is the wind.
6. soup and hot drinks inside the building women to the local mushers offer.
7. falling are big wind and a strong snowflakes blowing is.

Lösungen

Chapter 1:

1. Key words

1b) someone who does criminal things to stop other people from doing something
2c) a detective
3c) a person who drives a sled with dogs

2. Who's who?

1d) Francis Studstill
2c) Baxter Norsworthy
3b) Jared Fox
4a) Carol Ford

Detective Question 1:

Carol thinks the saboteur wants money.
Der Gewinner des Rennens kann mit Werbeverträgen viel Geld verdienen. Carol nimmt an, dass der Saboteur diese Werbeverträge und das damit verbundene Geld haben möchte.

3. Fill in the blanks

1. The sled dog race starts in **Dawson** and finishes in **Fairbanks.**
2. Four mushers cannot take part in the race because they or their dogs are **ill/sick.**
3. Carol's old camera team got **food poisoning** after they ate some cookies.
4. The winner of the race will do **advertising** for "Kodiak Sports" or "Apollo Dog-food".

Chapter 2:

4. Thief!

1. Somebody stole a bucket full of **gold** and a **bag** from the museum.
2. Carol says the thief could not leave Dawson because there was a **blizzard** on the night he stole the bag.
3. Now, the thief can't leave because the **police** are checking every car that leaves the town.
4. Carol is angry because nobody cares about the **sabotage/saboteur** anymore, because they are thinking about the stolen gold.

5. Gold!

1c) nugget, 2d) gold digger/prospector, 3e) valuable, 4b) gold mine, 5a) exhibition

Detective Question 2:

The thief may have needed something to carry the gold, or he was interested in the bag because of its history.
Zum einen brauchte der Dieb einen Behälter für das Gold, wobei es aber eher unwahrscheinlich ist, dass dies der Hauptgrund war. Zum anderen hatte die Tasche historischen Wert, weil sie dem berühmten Schriftsteller Jack London gehörte.

Chapter 3:

6. What's wrong?

Mr Woodland is a sponsor for the race. He is also the man who owns ~~the bag~~ which was stolen from the museum. (*Mr Woodland owns the gold, not the bag*) When he was young, he was ~~a teacher~~ (*an adventurer*).
Baxter Norworthy has a black coat and a ~~red~~ (*black*) sled. He is very ~~friendly and polite~~ (*rude*).
Candace Duskin is tall and blond. ~~She is the only woman in the race.~~ (*There are two women in the race, Candace Duskin and Francis Studstill*)

7. Word Chain
musher – Schlittenhundeführer; psychic – übersinnlich (adj.), Medium (noun); prospector – Goldsucher; artifact – Gegenstand, Artefakt; embarrassed – verlegen; cheer – jubeln; loss – Verlust; crowded – überfüllt

Detective Question 3:
Justus wants a list of all the people who might be saboteurs.

Chapter 4:

8. Camping equipment
Mögliche Antworten:
tent, sleeping bag, energy bars, fire starter, matches, torch, flashlight, mugs, gas cooker, coffee, teabags, water bottles

9. Animal world
moose, jackrabbit, owl
Bob fürchtet auch, dass ein Bär in der Nähe ist, dies ist aber unwahrscheinlich, da Bären Winterschlaf machen.

Detective Question 4:
Duane Carpenter is good-looking and Carol is very friendly to him and wants to travel with him.

Chapter 5:

10. Ways to say "say"

1. "Bob, be careful!" Carol **shouts.**
2. "It's very cold today," Duane Carpenter **says** to Justus.
3. "Good morning. Did you sleep well?" Francis **greets** boys when they climb out of their tents.
4. Peter **asks,** "Has anyone seen my sleeping bag?"
5. "Yes, it's on the ski-doo," Bob **answers.**
6. "Today, we will drive to the Yukon river," Carol **tells** the boys.
7. "When electrons collide with atoms of the upper atmosphere of the earth you get Northern lights," Justus **explains** to his friends.

11. Detective work

Es gibt keine einzelne richtige Antwort, da deine eigene Meinung gefragt ist.

12. Similar but different

1. If you steal something or murder someone, that's a **crime.**
2. When you do not know who has committed the crime, everybody who behaves strangely is **suspicious.**
3. A **suspect** is a person who you think possibly committed the crime.
4. If you think someone is a criminal, you **suspect** him.
5. A **criminal** is someone who has committed a crime.

13. Rules for Detectives

1b) The Three Investigators find out that the winner of the race will get lots of money by doing advertising for the sponsors.

2a) The Three Investigators ask Jelena to look up Duane Carpenter and the mushers on the internet.

3c) Peter decides to watch Baxter Norsworthy

Detective Question 5:

Peter thinks nice people are innocent and rude, unfriendly people must be guilty.

Peter mag Baxter Norsworthy nicht und denkt, dass er der Saboteur sein muss, da er unhöflich und rücksichtslos ist. Er ist viel zu subjektiv. Das wird noch klarer, als er sagt, dass Candace Duskin nicht die Saboteurin sein kann, weil sie nett und ***hübsch*** *ist.*

Chapter 6:

14. Disappointed

1. Peter, 2. Curtis Moylan, 3. Francis Studstill

15. On the track

falsche Fährte: palm – Palme, Handfläche; honey – Honig; sunburn – Sonnenbrand; skyscraper – Wolkenkratzer; drown – ertrinken

richtige Fährte: musher – Schlittenhundeführer; sled-dog – Schlittenhund; cabin – Hütte; nugget – Goldklumpen; prospector – Goldsucher; freeze to death – erfrieren; moose – Elch

Detective Question 6:

Curtis Moylan gets ill and Francis' dog Spooky does, too.

In beiden Fällen könnte es sich um Sabotage handeln, da es möglich ist, dass sowohl Curtis Moylan als auch Spooky vergiftet wurden.

Chapter 7:

16. The best word

1. When Peter sees the trail of blood he feels **shocked/scared.**
2. Bob worries that there is a **wolf/bear** in the woods.
3. After the attack, Candace Duskin looks **pale/ill.**
4. Duane Carpenter asks many questions and seems to be **excited.**

17. Ice-cold

sn-owy, exc-ited, sne-ak, uncons-cious, sab-oteur, inst-ead, ches-t, footpri-nts, diz-zy, band-aid, spo-oky, bloodsta-ined

Detective Question 7:

Baxter Norsworthy, Jared Fox and Gordon Hoke had the chance to attack Candace.

Baxter Norsworthy ist verdächtig, da er die Hütte verlassen hat und weggefahren ist. Jared Fox und Gordon Hoke haben beide kein Alibi, da sie in einer anderen Hütte geschlafen haben. Sie hatten also die Möglichkeit, Candace Duskin zu überfallen.

Chapter 8:

18. Scrambled Letters

1. poison, 2. map, 3. weapon, 4. gold, 5. clothes

19. Investigation

1. False, Baxter Norsworthy didn't poison Spooky. 2. true; 3. False, Duane Carpenter lied to us about his camera. 4. False, Francis Studstill was asleep in the Three Investigator's cabin when Miss Duskin was attacked. 5. False, the Three Investigators want to check the mushers and the photographer, Mr Carpenter.

Detective Question 8:

Duane Carpenter says his camera is a special camera that does not take blurred pictures in the dark. This is not true, it's a normal camera.
Bonus Question: Einige Ideen, was wohl in Baxters Kiste sein könnte, findest du in Übung **15**, siehe oben.

Chapter 9:

20. Snow and Cold Vocabulary

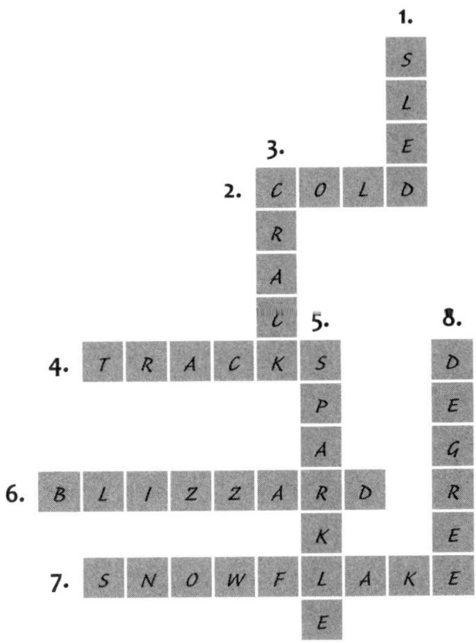

Across:
2. cold
4. tracks
6. blizzard
7. snowflake

Down:
1. sled
3. crack
5. sparkle
8. degree

Detective Question 9:
He thinks the men are from Beaver Falls because they wear orange jackets.
Es ist durchaus möglich, dass dies die Männer aus Beaver Falls sind, aber es könnten genau so gut andere Männer sein, die auch orange Jacken tragen.

Chapter 10:

21. Dog Vocab
Change to different answers for picture exercise

1. tail, 2. howl, 3. growl, 4. bark, 5. paw

Detective Question 10:
When they are frightened, the dogs whine, tuck their tails between their legs and the fur at their neck stands up.
They are probably scared of a wild animal.

Chapter 11:

22. What's the right answer?
1b) To call for help if you are at sea or in a lonely place.
2c) Mess with him.
3a) They howl.

Detective Question 11:
Jared Fox says he does not want Peter to spill any of the fire starter because it is a dangerous chemical.

Chapter 12:

23. Complete the sentence

1d) It's possible that Duane Carpenter is a criminal because he is lying about his job and maybe also about his name.

2b) Gordon Hoke probably wants to win the race very much because it's his last race.

3a) Candace Duskin might try to win by sabotage because the winner gets the advertising contract.

4c) Jared Fox might be trying to win the race by unfair means because he is always unlucky and never wins.

24. What a terrible mess!

1. accident – Unfall; 2. sabotage – Sabotage; 3. Mountain Girls – Name einer TV-Serie: Mädchen der Berge; 4. photographer – Fotograf; 5. Beaver Falls – Ortsname; 6. retire – in Ruhestand treten

Detective Question 12:

Duane is probably not the saboteur because he is not taking part in the race. He also has an alibi for the night Candace Duskin was attacked.

Da Duane Carpenter nicht am Rennen teilnimmt, kann er auch nichts gewinnen. Es kann ihm also egal sein, wer gewinnt. (Es sei denn, er ist mit einem der Hundeschlittenfuehrer verbündet und hilft ihm/ihr.) In der Nacht, in der Candace Duskin überfallen wird, schläft er in der gleichen Hütte wie die drei ???, hat also ein Alibi.

Chapter 13:

25. Bob's not perfect

1. Candace Duskin is the saboteur, she tried to ~~**brake**~~ (break) Baxter Norsworthy's sled.
2. ~~**Their**~~ (There) is a stuffed pig in the blue box.
3. Justus wants to ~~**proof**~~ (prove) that Candace Duskin is the saboteur.
4. Jared Fox hit Candace Duskin because he thought she wanted to ~~**steel**~~ (steal) the gold.
5. The First ~~**Investigetor**~~ (Investigator) is going to set a trap for Miss Duskin.

Detective Question 13:

Baxter can't be the saboteur because he smelled so strongly of his deodorant that Candace would have recognized him.

Baxter Norsworthy roch zum Zeitpunkt als Candace Duskin überfallen wurde noch stark nach seinem Deodorant, und sie hätte ihn an diesem Geruch erkannt. Wie auffällig der Geruch ist, demonstriert Justus mit seinem kleinen Experiment an Peter.

Chapter 14:

26. Scrambled sentences

1. Justus and Peter want to follow Jared Fox.
2. The museum hired George Bennett to find the thief.
   Oder: To find the thief, the museum hired George Bennett.
3. George Bennett says what Peter and Justus are doing is dangerous.
4. Bob, Carol and George Bennett will try to help Justus and Peter

Detective Question 14:
George Bennett pretended to be a photographer called Duane Carpenter because he is a detective hired by an insurance company. *George Bennett ermittelt im Zusammenhang mit dem Diebstahl in Dawsons Museum, will aber natürlich nicht offiziell als Detektiv auftreten.*

Chapter 15:

27. Find the mistakes

Many houses in the ghost town have broken windows and roofs. The house where Jared Fox is ~~is much smaller~~ (is much bigger) than the other houses. The house is ~~on top of~~ (built into) a hill. There is a long balcony several feet above the ground. The balcony is ~~very new and not at all dangerous~~ (very old and unsound).

28. Detective's work

1. crime; 2. saboteur; 3. suspicion; 4. evidence; 5. innocent

Detective Question 15:
Peter climbs onto the balcony because he wants to hear what the men in the house are saying. *Peter ist der Meinung, dass Justus nicht auf den Balkon klettern sollte, weil er zu schwer und zu unsportlich ist, und klettert deshalb selbst auf den Balkon.*

Chapter 16:

29. Combine

1g) make sure, 2c) what a shame, 3b) take a deep breath, 4f) point a gun at someone, 5e) lay down the weapon, 6d) freeze to death, 7a) ask for help

Detective Question 16:

Mr Woodland says that nobody will believe the boys, so it is not a problem to let them go.
Es ist aber durchaus möglich, dass er nur bereit ist, sie gehen zu lassen, weil er der Meinung ist, dass sie sowieso im Sturm umkommen werden. Zu Fuß in einem Schneesturm in der Wildnis sind ihre Überlebenschancen nicht sehr gut.

Chapter 17:

30. Noises

Im Text: wail, growl

Weitere Vorschläge: howl (heulen), screech (kreischen), cackle (wie eine Hexe lachen), grunt (grunzen), roar (wie ein Löwe brüllen), breathe loudly (laut atmen), break twigs to make crackling noises (Zweige zerbrechen, um knackende Geräusche zu machen), groan (stöhnen, ächzen)

Detective Question 17:

Bob gets the idea because Justus, who knows that Bob can hear him, talks about monsters very loudly.

Chapter 18:

31. Complete the sentences

1. Justus **knew/proved** that Candace Duskin was the saboteur.
2. Candace tried to **deny** that she was guilty, but the black **stains/ marks** on her hands were evidence against her.
4. The police will **arrest** her.
5. She is very **angry** with The Three Investigators and does not want their **card**.
6. The Three Investigators are proud because they solved both **cases**.

Detective Question 18:

Candace Duskin got the paste onto her hands when she tried to sabotage Baxter's things.

Justus hatte seine spezielle Paste auf Baxters Kiste, seinen Schlitten und seine Wasserflasche geschmiert, so dass Candace bei ihrem Sabotageversuch etwas davon auf die Hände bekam.

Chapter 19:

32. Whoops!

To find out who the saboteur is, The Three Investigators collect ~~flowers~~ **evidence** and look out for ~~nice~~ **suspicious** behaviour.

The thief ~~looked~~ **broke** into the museum and took a bag of ~~bread~~ **gold**.

Jared Fox helped the ~~murderer~~ **thief** to get the gold out of Dawson.

When Justus and Peter discover that he is ~~a suspect~~ **guilty/a criminal**, he points a ~~stick~~ **gun** at them.

At the end of the investigation, The Three Investigators find out that Candace Duskin is ~~innocent~~ **guilty**. They decide that she should be sent to ~~the beach~~ **prison**.

When Duane Carpenter sees the criminals, he shouts: '~~Move~~ **Freeze**!' and tells them to ~~keep~~ **drop** their weapons.

33. Detective Vocab

1. investigator, 2.case, 4.arrest, 5.criminal, 6.thief, 7. evidence, 8. detective

34. Tidy up!

1. The blond woman looks at him with anger in her eyes.
2. It's already dark when they all arrive at Little Jackson, the next town.
3. Peter isn't there anymore.
4. They are keeping an eye on her until the police arrive.
5. There is a lot of snow on the streets and the wind is strong.
6. Inside the building local women offer soup and hot drinks to the mushers.
7. A strong wind is blowing and big snowflakes are falling.

Detective Question 19:

It's up to you, the correct answer is the one you choose, because we are asking for your opinion!